# Secret Societies

## THE HIDDEN MASTERS CONTROLLING OUR WORLD

## Welcome to the Brotherhood

Karin Gutman

Published by
Kandour Limited
Monticello House
45 Russell Square
London WC1B 4JP
United Kingdom

First published 2007

10 9 8 7 6 5 4 3 2 1

Jacket Design: Alex Ingr

Design Layout: Michael Lomax

Art Editor: David Fraser

Production Manager: Carol Titchener

Sales & Editorial Manager: Karen Lomax

Author: Karin Gutman

Text Copyright © Kandour Limited 2007

Design Copyright © Kandour Limited 2007

Printed and bound in Singapore

ISBN 13: 978-1-905741-50-2

A catalogue record of this book is available from the British Library

# SECRET SOCIETIES

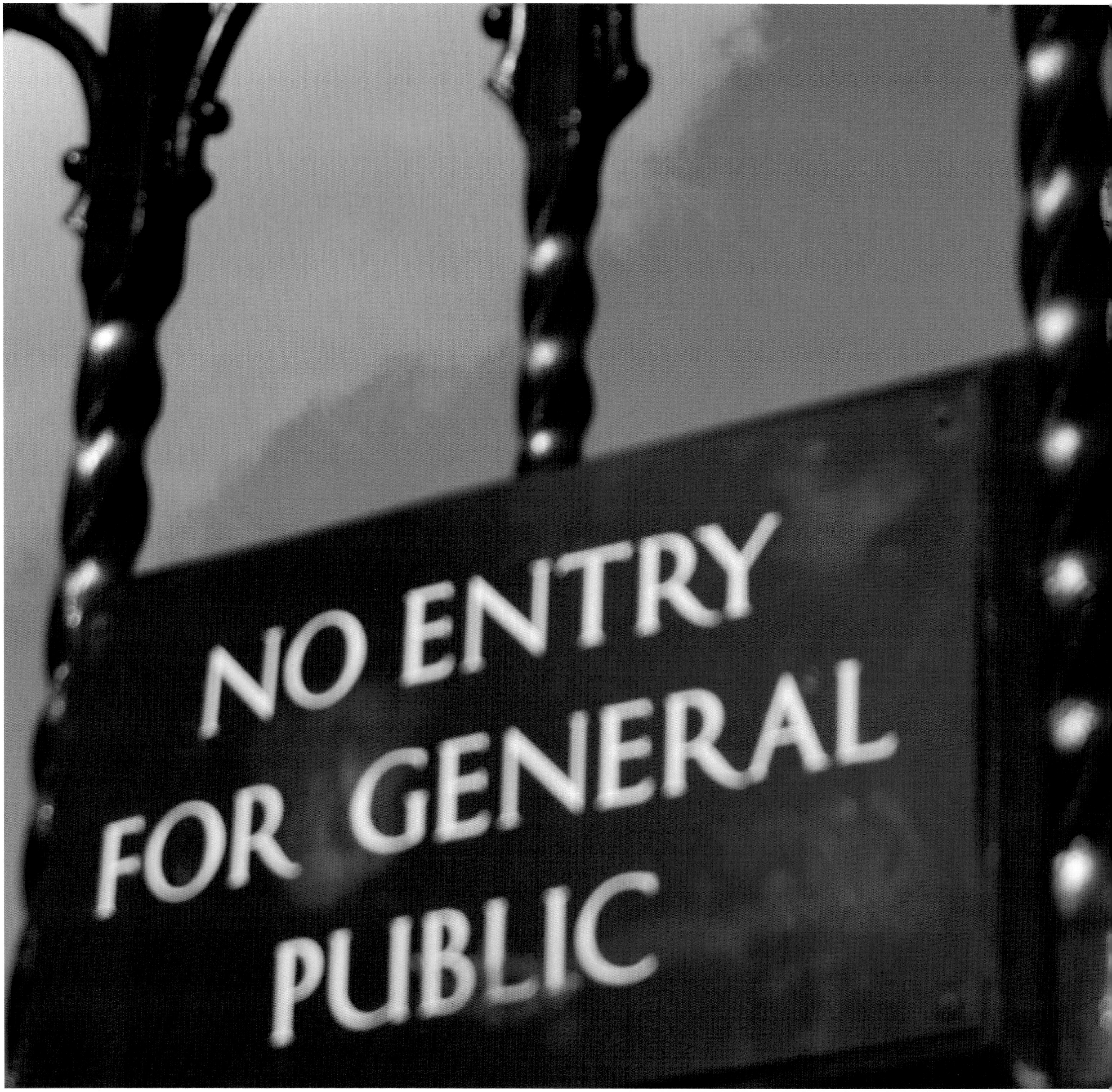
NO ENTRY
FOR GENERAL
PUBLIC

# CONTENTS

><-+-<>-<>-<+-><

*Cryptex with a secret message inside*

# INTRODUCTION:

# SECRET SOCIETIES

WHAT IS THE TRUTH BEHIND SECRET
SOCIETIES? DO CLANDESTINE GROUPS INDEED
EXIST? STRATEGIZING BEHIND CLOSED DOORS,
MASTERMINDING PLOTS TO TAKE OVER
THE WORLD?

Webster's New Collegiate Dictionary, 1975, defines a secret society as "any of various oath-bound societies often devoted to brotherhood, moral discipline, and mutual assistance." This characterization hardly suggests anything threatening. More often, people associate secret societies with organizations shrouded in mystery, promoting subversive agendas and requiring members to conceal their activities from outsiders. Distinguished by symbols and signs, mystical ceremonies and vows of silence, many claim to hold the keys to secret truths. Even though some societies openly declare their roster of members and meeting locations, the invitations to join tend to be exclusive, if not highly selective. New inductees are rumored to perform initiation rites and rituals that include oaths demanding unbending loyalty.

As depicted in the pages that follow, some organizations are renowned for criminal activity, while the majority present themselves as benign fraternal groups, functioning on behalf of a greater good. What, then, is the nature of their secrecy? Anything deliberately concealed begets mistrust and suspicion in the general public—cultivating paranoia. History reveals that some groups were originally forced underground for self-preservation, while others appear to be bona fide hoaxes now a part of our collective mythology. Still, the conspiracy buffs claim that among them are wolves acting in the guise of sheep, worthy of further investigation.

CHAPTER 1:

# HASHSHASHIN (THE ASSASSINS)

>━┤◆━○━◆┤━<

A GROUP THAT HAVE SINCE BECOME
SYNONYMOUS WITH KILLERS, THE ASSASSINS
BEGAN AS AN 11TH-CENTURY RELIGIOUS SECT IN
THE MOUNTAINS OF NORTHERN PERSIA.

>━┤◆━○━◆┤━<

The word "assassin" stems from Hassassin—a follower of Hassan ibn Sabbah. A leader of the Ismaili Muslims, Hassan was known as the "Old Man on the Mountain." In 1090 AD he took control of the Alamut fortress atop the Alborz Mountains in the barren wilderness of northern Persia. From there, he carried out a reign of terror, founding one of the most chilling secret societies known as *Hashshashin*, or the Assassins.

Many believe this Islamic sect may have been the first terrorists. It grew out of a schism between the Shiites and

Sunnis when Prophet Mohammed died. The two groups disagreed on how his successor would be named. The Shiites further divided into splinter groups, out of which produced the Ismailis, a particularly violent faction. Hassan assumed authority of its Nizari branch, claiming to possess a direct connection to the Prophet and his secret wisdom. His followers, in turn, became his faithful disciples—and ruthless killers.

Hassan made assassination both an art and an education. At his mountaintop headquarters, he created a training base to breed an arsenal of deadly agents. He attracted young men, often from poverty-stricken families, whose malleable minds suited his techniques. These devotees, or *fidayeen*, underwent rigorous

*The Holy Koran*

## "SELF-SACRIFICE WAS PART OF THE ORDER'S SILENT OATH"

formal instruction. Through secret oaths, mysterious rites and isolation from the world, the men were indoctrinated to become trained assassins. Hassan's primary strategy was infiltration. The *fidayeen* learned the art of blending into communities where the target was located by becoming well-versed in disguises, languages, and court etiquette. They became proficient in the dress and manners of monks, merchants, and soldiers—anyone they needed to impersonate in order to carry out their missions.

Hassan led inductees through an extensive initiation process. He extracted from the teachings of the *Abode of Learning*, an Ismaili instruction program in Cairo, which consisted of a nine-stage process. Hassan reduced the steps to the mystical number seven. Like the *Abode*, his program used a concentric structure, whereby the epicenter of power and knowledge remained concealed. "It is the classic method of securing allegiance to a group's cause, by gradually building a foundation of unquestioned obedience," writes John Lawrence, author of *Secret Societies: Inside the World's Most Notorious Organizations*. The teachings destroyed the concept of organized religion. Instead, Hassan brainwashed the men into believing that he singularly possessed the divine truth. The new initiates believed that by accessing Hassan's secret knowledge, they would gain hidden powers.

Hassan further entranced the initiates with a unique ritual. According to legend, Hassan constructed a secret garden and furnished it with all the delights of Paradise. The chosen men were then drugged, a few at a time, and taken to this oasis at night. When they awoke,

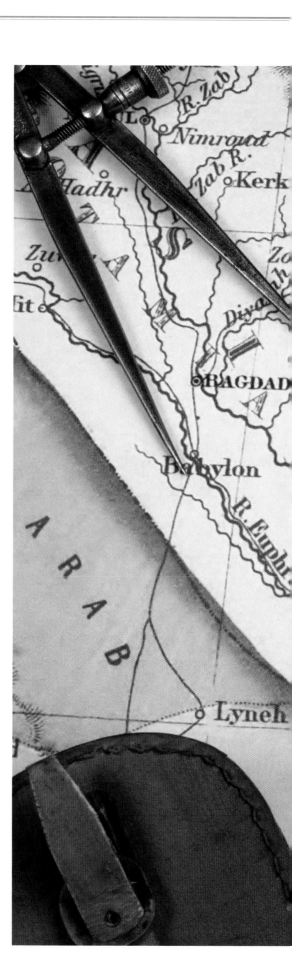

Islamic symbol of Mohammed

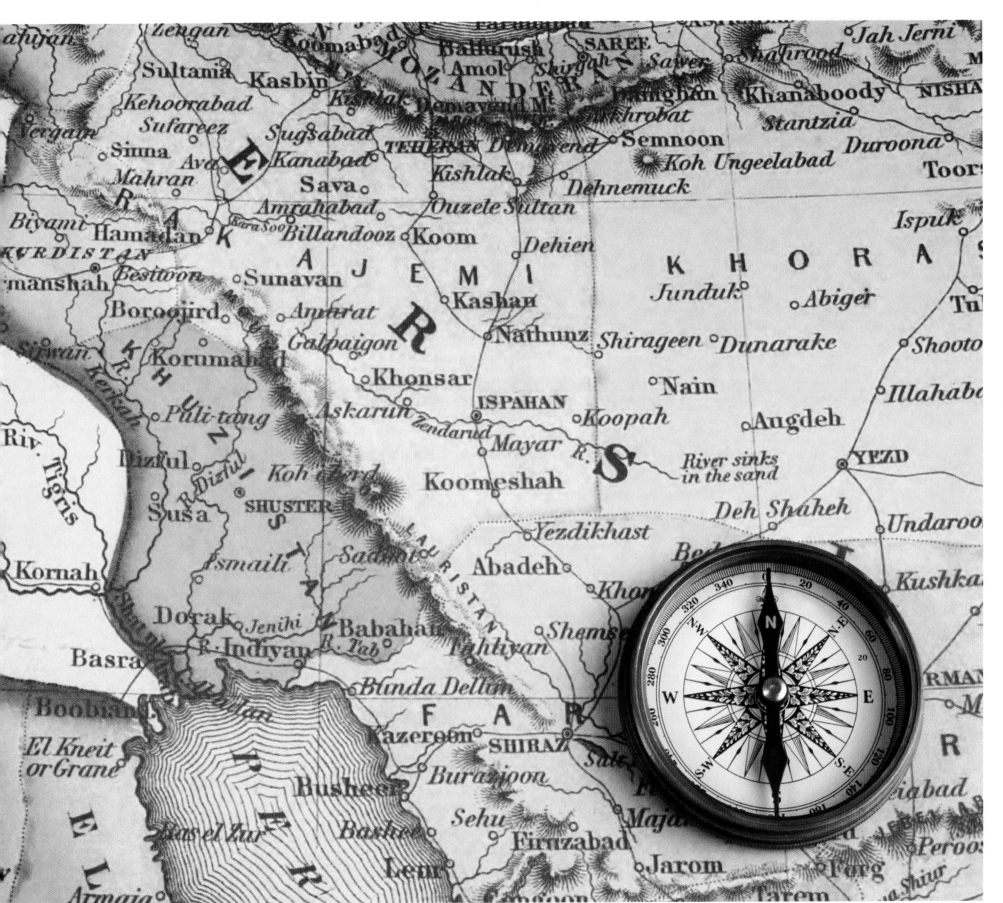

*The Alamut fortress was located atop the Alborz Mountains in northern Persia*

The dagger was the Assassin's weapon of choice

they experienced an earthly ecstasy, surrounded by beautiful women. "They truly believed themselves to be in paradise," wrote Marco Polo in 1273 of the tales he had heard. "And these damsels were always with them in songs and great entertainments; they received everything they asked for, so that they would never have left that garden of their own will." After being pleasured by these scantily clad women, known as *houris*, the men were drugged again and then transferred to a dungeon. Hassan addressed the men in this squalid dwelling, telling them that Allah had given them a preview of Paradise. He explained that they could again experience this nirvana, provided that they submitted to his orders in blind obedience.

After completing their training, the *fidayeen* were sent on missions where they discreetly positioned themselves and awaited further instruction from their Master. Once they received their cue, the assassins acted promptly. One day they were working as lowly peasants, and the next day instantly transformed into fierce warriors. They murdered their victims in public, often in mosques. This technique bolstered the sect's terrifying reputation. Typically, the dagger was the weapon of choice, to ensure execution rather than escape. The assassins were prudent when killing their target, seeking to eliminate him without any additional casualties or loss of innocent life. The killers would then willingly surrender to their own deaths, usually at the hands of the victim's bodyguards. Self-sacrifice was part of the Order's silent oath.

Hassan's techniques proved highly effective. The followers, as well as their families, were fully committed to his cause. The phrase "as faithful as an Assassin" grew out of the *fidayeens'* unwavering deference to their Master's commands. The assignments usually singled out foes of Hassan, aiming to achieve either military or political ends. The men believed their acts to be necessary and for the greater good. They carried out their missions with the noblest intentions.

During its 166-year reign, the Hashshashin successfully executed many high-profile assassinations. In 1092 an assassin dressed as a Sufi took out the illustrious Muslim leader Nizam-el-Mulk. A series of mysterious murders followed, thereby establishing the Assassins as

*Marco Polo visited Alamut in 1273*

*Hashshashin often murdered their victims in mosques*

a deadly force. A century later, the machine had proven to be well oiled and exceptionally deceptive. In 1191, Christian de Montferrat became the new King of Jerusalem, determined to drive out all Muslim forces. Three assassins innocently appeared at his door in the guise of Christian monks. After persuading the guards to put down their swords, they withdrew their daggers and cut Montferrat to pieces. True to tradition, the killers did not try to escape afterwards, but instead submitted to their own gruesome deaths.

Over time, fear of the Assassins grew. They were known to be ruthless and unpredictable. Public criticisms gradually disappeared in order to avoid becoming a target of Hassan's brutal machine. Hassan increased fortifications around Alamut, renaming it "Eagle's Nest," and expanded his operations into Syria. The cooperation of Muslim allies, such as the Aleppo ruler Ridwan, permitted the Assassins to erect more fortresses. At the same time, an increasing number of clandestine sleeper cells were dispatched to remote communities, each one harboring secret agents.

When Hassan died in 1124, the Order showed no signs of waning. It only grew stronger. Hassan's last words would forever echo in their minds, inspiring future leaders: "Remember, nothing is true; everything is permitted." Between 1090 and 1256 the Order operated under eight different Grand Masters. Each leader proved fiercer than ever, injecting terror into the hearts of Crusaders. Rachid-al-Din Sinan was one of the most famous, residing atop Masyad in Syria. The Grand Masters were known to demonstrate their authority to anyone who questioned their power. During the Crusades, Henry de Champagne paid a visit to Alamut, having accepted the Master Dai-el-Kebir's invitation to view the fortress. With a simple wave of his hand, the Kebir ordered his

☒ *Al Qaeda explosion*

sentinels to jump from the towers to their deaths. They performed this act without hesitation, leaving Henry incredulous. What sort of man would jump to a senseless end at the whim of his Master? More importantly, how could such power by a leader be rivaled?

Alamut posed a threat, and there were many attempts to destroy it. However, there was only one pathway up the mountain, making Alamut nearly invincible. Saladin, the general of Islamic armies, invaded the fortress in 1176. After several attempts made on his own life, he decided that the cult must be destroyed. The Hashshashin proposed a truce. Saladin agreed to back down his forces, on the condition that the Hashshashin would no longer make him

a target for assassination. Years later, Saladin even convinced King Richard II of England to preserve territories belonging to the Assassins.

Using these fear tactics, the sect managed to survive nearly 200 years of persecution, successfully maintaining the fortress between the 11th and 13th centuries. They held their ground in both Iran and Syria against overwhelming hostile forces, including the Abbasids, Saljuk Turks and Crusaders. "Hassan's contribution to the art of assassination was that by careful selection, training, and inspiration he developed the practice into a sacred ritual and the prime weapon of a small state waging war against a great power," wrote Enno Franzius, author of *History of the Order of Assassins.*

☒ *Saladin (Salahuldin Al-Ayyubi)*

15

*Memorial honoring the September 11, 2001 suicide attacks*

*Memorial dedicated to the assassination of Israeli Prime Minister Yitzhak Rabin*

"Thus, Alamut became the greatest training center of fanatical politico-religious assassins the world has known."

It was not until the Mongols invaded Alamut in 1256 that the Hashshashin were effectively destroyed. Hulagua Khan attacked the fortress and massacred most of the sect members. The Syrian branch of the sect suffered a similar fate at the hands of the Egyptian Mamluks. The remaining cult members scattered across northern Syria, Persia, and India. Their population today is estimated to be 150,000.

They call themselves Thojas or Mowlas and acknowledge Aga Khan as their titular head, a descendant of the last Ismaili Grand Master of Alamut.

The Ismaili library was destroyed during the Alamut siege, wiping out the sect's original records. The Hashshashin, nonetheless, left behind a considerable legacy. By the middle of the 14th century, the word "assassin" had become a familiar term to describe a professional murder, even though the Order was no longer a viable force in the Middle East. Ever since, the cult

has continued to inspire assassins worldwide, currently carrying out missions on the streets of Baghdad, Beirut, and Tel Aviv.

The similarities between the Hashshashin and the modern-day Al Qaeda group are striking. Operating under the direction of Osama bin Laden, the Al Qaeda operatives roam the hills of Afghanistan and threaten civilians across the globe. This terrorist organization employs similar practices to the Hashshashin, including infiltration, sleeper cells, and terror tactics. Al Qaeda's primary objective is to eradicate infidels, and its members are prepared to die for their cause. Using men as instruments of revenge has its roots in the cult of the Assassins. A "fidayeen attack" now refers to Muslim fanatics who perform suicide bombings as their weapon of choice, like the men who flew into the World Trade Center on September 11, 2001.

The story of the Hashshashin offers an important insight for our time, given the threat of terrorism that is now upon us. 

*Memorial honoring the September 11, 2001 suicide attacks*

# CHAPTER 2:

# KNIGHTS TEMPLAR

"THE WARRIORS ARE GENTLER THAN LAMBS AND FIERCER THAN LIONS," SAID BERNARD DE CLARIVAUX ABOUT THE KNIGHTS TEMPLAR, "WEDDING THE MILDNESS OF THE MONK WITH THE VALOR OF THE KNIGHT."

Templar insignia, displaying a white mantle with a red cross

The Knights Templar was among the most famous Christian military orders during medieval times. They are implicated in numerous mysteries and are allegedly the guardians of the Holy Grail. Their spectacular demise, brought down by torture and executions, is the subject of much debate to this very day both within the Church and in popular culture. The novel *Holy Blood, Holy Grail* spins tales about the Templars that seeded the colossal success of *The Da Vinci Code*. Now two follow-up thrillers, *The Last Templar* and *The Templar Legacy*, have established themselves on The New York Times bestseller list.

What is the truth behind the Templar legacy? And why is it so compelling? To answer these questions, we must turn back the clock to uncover the precise story of these fabled knights…

The year is 1050. Pilgrimages to the Holy Land of Jerusalem had become a duty for Christians. Although the routes were well defined, the two-year trek required a journey across rough terrain and hostile territory. The Islamic armies routinely slaughtered the pilgrims, sometimes by the hundreds, as they made their way from Jaffa to their point of destination. In response, Pope Urban II declared a Holy War in 1096, launching the first of nine crusades. Fearless knights led the charge, successfully capturing the city of Jerusalem in 1099. As good men in service to their feudal lords and to God, the knights became defenders of the Christian faith. They had made vows of poverty, chastity, and obedience, while also embracing their duties as valiant warriors. Surprisingly, the knights' pious religious behaviour and ruthless martial exploits were remarkably compatible.

*Old city wall in Jerusalem*

In spite of their successes, the crusaders struggled to establish an effective military and political structure to protect their conquests. Bandits still abounded in the outer country, intensifying the danger to the abundant inflow of Europeans. Gerard de Martignes established a hospital to shelter the pilgrims, thereby founding the Hospitaliers. An adjoining marketplace to trade with the pilgrims ignited a rich source of profit, attracting others to this commercial opportunity. The Hospitaliers' effort to care for the pilgrims by providing them safety and comfort appealed to the knights' spiritual goals. The warriors regarded this assistance as a way to elevate their status in the eyes of their feudal lords, and more importantly, in the eyes of God. They longed to put aside their military objectives for more chivalrous endeavors.

And so, in 1119, nine knights gathered to form a monastic order for the protection of these pilgrims. And voilà… the Knights Templar were born. French knight Hugues de Payens and his relative Godfrey de Saint-Omer, veterans of the first crusade, approached King Baldwin II of Jerusalem with their intention. The King fully embraced the idea and granted the Templars headquarters on Temple Mount in the captured Al Aqsa Mosque. An aura of mystique surrounded the temple, as it was believed to be the ruins of the ancient Temple of Solomon. This location inspired the Order's official name: The Poor Fellow-Soldiers of Christ and of the Temple of Solomon, or more

☒ *During the Crusades, the knights protected pilgrims on their way to the Holy Land of Jerusalem. Above: A map of Jaffa and Jerusalem*

commonly known as the "Knights Templar" or "Order of the Temple."

As membership grew, the Order blossomed into a fraternal organization of public status, requiring that a formal structure be imposed. Hugues de Payens became the first Grand Master of the Order. Appointed for life, the Grand Master oversaw the military efforts and financial assets of the Templars. Underneath Payens, the hierarchical division broke down into three levels: 1) the aristocratic knights, 2) lower-born sergeants, and 3) the clergy, or chaplains. The knights were equipped with heavy cavalry, while the sergeants focused largely on administrative duties, maintaining only one or two horses each. The chaplains naturally supported the Order's spiritual needs as ordained priests.

The rigid initiation process established the Templars' reputation as a "secret society." Acceptance into the order was a profound commitment and involved a secret ceremony. The candidates were also required to pledge allegiance and undergo a serious boot camp. Few details would ever be exposed surrounding the mysterious rituals, but it is known that members were required to turn over all their assets to the order. A specific code of conduct was outlined in the Latin Rule, established by Hugues de Payens and Bernard de Clairvaux, a patron of the Templars. Its 72 clauses defined the ideal behavior for the Knights, such as the types of robes they were to wear and how many horses they could have. Knights were to eat their meals in silence, eat no more than three times a week, and have no physical contact of any kind with women. As the order grew, even more guidelines were added.

The Pope officially endorsed the Order at the Council of Troyes in Champagne in 1129, at the behest of Bernard de Clairvaux. A nephew of one of the knights, Clairvaux wrote

*The metal shield of a Crusader*

The Knights Templar established their headquarters in the Al Asqa Mosque on Temple Mount

persuasively on behalf of the order seeking a formal blessing. He described the Knights as men "eager for victory—not fame; for battle not for pomp; who abhor wasteful speech, unnecessary action, unmeasured laughter, gossip and chatter, as they despise all vain things; who in spite of their being many, live in one house according to one rule, with one soul and one heart." Ten years later, Pope Innocent II exempted the Order from obedience to local laws. This ruling meant that the Templars could pass freely through all borders, were not required to pay any taxes, and were exempt from all authority except that of the Pope.

While at first the knights relied on donations to support their cause, they soon became doused with riches, now graced with papal recognition. The status and allure of the Order exploded, making the Templars the favorite charity across Europe. The benevolent knights were awarded extensive lands for their works, along with businesses and booty from their conquests. Ironically, the Knights Templar emblem, depicted two knights on a single horse

*Al Asqa Mosque*

*Templar cross on a medieval castle*

## "THE TEMPLARS BUILT A FORMIDABLE ECONOMIC INFRASTRUCTURE ACROSS EUROPE"

emphasizing their vow of poverty-no longer reflected their reality.

The Templars went on to build a formidable economic infrastructure across Europe—essentially all of Christendom, creating an early banking system. Although the primary mission of the Order was military, only a small number were actually on the front lines. The non-warriors took on administrative duties, helping to manage the ever-growing organism

that rivaled the power of kings. Here's how it would work: If a nobleman were interested in joining the Crusades, he would place all his valuable assets into the hands of the Templars while he was gone. He would thereby receive a document of credit that he would present upon arrival in the Holy Land. This proof of credit permitted him to access his personal funds at the other end. This rudimentary checking service not only improved the safety of pilgrims, now

*The official seal of the Knights Templar displays two knights on a single horse, emphasizing the vow of poverty*

"TO DIE IN COMBAT WAS A GREAT HONOR, ASSURING THE KNIGHTS A PLACE IN HEAVEN"

less of a target for thieves, but also contributed to the Templar coffers. The Order then used this money to buy and manage farms and vineyards, to build churches and castles, and to enjoy their own fleet of ships—not to mention owning the entire island of Cyprus! The Templars arguably qualify as the world's first multinational corporation.

All the while, the Templars were a fearsome force on the battlefield. The knights wore with pride their white mantles emblazoned with a red cross, a symbol of martyrdom. To die in combat was considered a great honor, assuring the knights a place in heaven. One of

their most famous victories occurred during the Battle of Montgisard in 1177 where 500 Templar knights defeated Saladin's army of some 26,000 soldiers. However, around the same time, the crusading tides started to turn. The Islamic army proved to be more cohesive than the divisive dynamics among its Christian counterparts. The Templars were often at odds with other Christian orders such as the Knights Hospitalier and Teutonic Knights. Several disastrous battles led to the pivotal Battle of the Horns of Hattin, resulting in the surrender of Jerusalem to Saladin in 1187. By 1244, the Holy Land would be fully in the hands of Islam, never again to be under Christian control.

This defeat landed the Templars in a serious crisis. What appeared to be an invincible order was now showing signs of weakness. In 1291, the Christians had been expelled from Palestine by the Mamluks of Egypt, which forced the Templars to relocate to Tortosa (in what is now Syria) to continue their Holy War. From there, the Templars moved again to their remaining and final base in Cyprus. Since Templar success had been closely allied with the Crusades, European support for the Order rapidly dwindled. Even so, the Templars were by now well integrated into the daily lives of Europeans, having established an extensive network of banks, businesses, and property. They also still enjoyed the freedoms granted to them by the Pope. However, without a battlefield and a clear purpose, the Templars began to arouse suspicions and tension among the nobility.

What followed was a summons from the new Pope, Clement V, based in France. He sent letters to both Templar Grand Master Jacques de Molay and Hospitalier Grand Master Fulk de Villaret, proposing the idea of merging the two orders in light of their faltering mission. While this prospect met with little enthusiasm, Molay made his way to visit the

Coat of arms bearing Templar crosses

*Cyprus, the last Templar stronghold*

*Notre Dame Cathedral in Paris, the site of the Templar executions*

*French King Philip 'the Fair'*

"A DEFECTED
TEMPLAR ACCUSED
THE ORDER OF
BLASPHEMOUS
RITUALS"

Pope in 1307 bringing with him 60 knights and loads of silver and gold. Meanwhile, the brewing rumors about the Templars' secret initiation ceremony escalated, and King Philip "the Fair" of France pressured the Pope to take action. A defected Templar, Squin de Flexian, intensified the negative perceptions by accusing the order of blasphemous rituals, including sodomy, idol worship, and spitting on crucifixes. It is unclear whether King Philip indeed felt threatened by these allegations, or rather, that he had his eye on the Templar fortunes. Regardless of the King's motivations, Pope Clement pursued the investigation and received a declaration of innocence from de Molay on behalf of his order.

A simple plea of virtue satisfied the Pope, but not King Philip. On October 13, 1307, the French King ordered the arrest of all Templar members in France. It is widely believed

*Effigy of a Templar Knight*

*Temple Church in London, made famous by* The Da Vinci Code, *was built in the 12th century as the English headquarters for the Knights Templar*

that the King then tortured the Templars into confessions, though many of them later recanted. While the general public found the charges difficult to believe, this situation created a major scandal in Paris and instigated outcries against the order. The Pope eventually submitted to the increasing pressure from the King, who now threatened military action, and ordered all the Christian monarchs across Europe to arrest the Templars. Coordinated raids took place, seizing all the Templar assets in the process. Tribunal hearings then followed to determine the Knights' guilt or innocence.

Five years later at the Council of Vienne, the Pope felt compelled to abolish the Order entirely, after nearly two hundred centuries of defending the Christian faith. All Templar assets were turned over to the Hospitaliers, and to its great shock, the public experienced the sudden disappearance of the Templars from their lives. What happened next elevated the Templars to their unique place in history. In March of 1314, Grand Master Jacques de Molay and his close colleague Geoffrey de Charney were burned to death at the stake. It is said that de Molay maintained his innocence until the very end, asking that his body face the Notre Dame Cathedral as the flames took hold. In the eyes of his compadres, he went down as a true martyr. According to legend, de Molay publicly declared that Pope Clement and King Philip would soon meet him before God. As fate would have it, the Pope died of colic a month later, and the King met his death in a hunting accident just a few months after that.

Today the Roman Catholic Church calls the persecutions unjust and attributes this event to the tremendous pressure the Pope must have felt from King Philip, in addition to the public controversy. The Church states that there was actually nothing wrong with the Order of the Knights Templar, a position that has helped

*Knights Templar Castle in Portugal*

shape the modern-day image of the knights as noble men who were sacrificed.

Although history has glorified these men, the persecutions at the time were real and deadly. The remaining members either merged with other orders such as the Knights Hospitaliers, or emigrated to less contentious regions such as the excommunicated country of Scotland. In Portugal, the Templars simply changed their name to the Knights of Christ. The true loyalists were forced underground, enhancing the intrigue around their tragic and dramatic end. Supposedly, on the evening of de Molay's execution, a unique piece of knowledge was transferred to the care of future generations, creating a fertile source of drama for popular novelists. The variations and speculations are endless. Some believe the Templar fortunes are hidden inside Rosslyn Chapel, a 15th century Episcopal Church in Scotland. Others claim that the chapel holds secret codes, only decipherable by a true Templar, which would then reveal the true location of the hidden treasure. Still others debunk the Rosslyn theory entirely, pointing instead to Oak Island for the pot of gold, located off the coast of Nova Scotia.

*Old door of Rosslyn Chapel*

*The Templar fortunes are reportedly hidden in Rosslyn Chapel*

The most fantastic legend, and perhaps the most well known, is the Templars' early connection to the Temple of Solomon. It is believed that the Templars found the Holy Grail or Arc of the Convenant while residing on Mount Temple. This holy relic is thought to have fomented the great Templar battles with Saladin's armies, provoking a tug-of-war game for the prized possession. The grail tales take many forms. In Arthurian legend, the hero of the Grail quest, Sir Galahad, was pictured bearing a shield with the cross of St. George, similar to Templar insignia. However, there is no mention of the Holy Grail, or anything like a grail relic, documented in the Templar inquisitions.

For those looking for some shred of real evidence, there is one celebrated artifact that may be linked to the Templars—the Shroud of Turin. In 1357, the shroud was first publicly displayed by the family of Geoffrey de Charney, the Templar who was burned at the stake with Molay. While the artifact's origins are still under debate, the linen cloth bears an image of a man who appears to have been traumatized in a manner consistent with crucifixion. For this reason, some believe that Jesus of Nazareth may have been wrapped inside of it when he was placed in his tomb. However, the carbon dating in fact indicates that the shroud was created between 1260 and 1390, a time period that includes the Templar executions.

And so, the Templar legacy lives on. The story of the secretive yet powerful medieval warriors trails behind it an aura of mystique and grandeur. As the character Casaubon says in Umberto Eco's satire *Foucault's Pendulum*, "The Templars have something to do with everything."

*Many believe the Knights Templar are the keepers of the Holy Grail*

*Instruments of mysticism and the occult (tarot cards, pentacle, crystal, wand, bell and flowers)*

# CHAPTER 3:

# ROSICRUCIANS

A SOCIETY SAID TO HAVE ITS ROOTS IN

14TH-CENTURY GERMANY, THE ROSICRUCIANS

CLAIM TO BE KEEPERS OF ANCIENT

SECRETS AND WISDOM

No documents exist to confirm its true authenticity. And yet, the legendary esoteric order of the Rosicrucians claims to be the keeper of ancient secrets and wisdom, assisting humanity in its spiritual development. Members profess the power to command spirits and render themselves invisible. Over time, the society's ambiguous origins have proven to be a part of its charm. Its 400-year evolution has inspired several modern-day operative groups—a testament that Rosicrucians are still thriving among us.

In the early 17th century, three publications catapulted the secret order into public consciousness: *The Fama Fraternitas of the Meritorious Order of the Rosy Cross* (1614), *The Confession of the Rosicrucian Fraternity* (1615) and *The Chymical Marriage of Christian Rosenkreuz* (1616)

According to Rosicrucian legend, the society began with Christian Rosenkrantz, a German born in 1378. *The Fama Fraternitas* was a curious pamphlet published in 1614 that told his story. At age 16, this young man set out for the Middle East, where he learned mystical teachings from Arabs and Egyptians. Upon returning to Germany in 1407, he founded the Rosicrucian Order. It was a society of like-minded people, eight persons in total, which he named The Fraternity of the Rose Cross, or Rose-Croix. The Order also built a temple called Spiritus Sanctus, which was completed in 1409. It is said that Christian Rosenkrantz died at the ripe old age of 150, his body entombed in the temple. As the story goes, his grave was rediscovered in 1604, thereby spawning a rebirth and spreading of the order.

The Fama manifesto outlined the six fundamental agreements among the Order's members: 1) They pledged to be healers, accepting no payment for their services; 2) They would dress according to the custom of

*Alchemy in motion (jinn from a bottle)*

the country where they lived; 3) They would meet annually at Spiritus Sanctus; 4) Each person was required to name his successor; 5) The letters "C.R" would serve as their seal; and 6) The fraternity would remain secret for 100 years. The Rose-Croix document also emphatically declared its terms for accepting new members: "whosoever shall earnestly, and from his heart, bear affection unto us, it shall be beneficial to him in goods, body, and soul; but he that is false-hearted, or only greedy of riches, the same first of all shall not be able in any manner of wise to hurt us, but bring himself to utter ruin and destruction."

The first two publications never revealed their authorship, offering little evidence that such a fraternity ever existed. Then, a third publication appeared in 1616 entitled *The Chymical Wedding of Christian Rosenkrantz*. This work follows Rosenkrantz through a mystical wedding, using an alchemical allegory to tell its story. A man by the name of Johann Valentin Andreae later revealed himself to be the author, a claim he made in his autobiography. It is thought that Andreae meant for his work to be a satire of alchemists, such as Paracelsus, and reportedly referred to it as "a jest, of little worth." Instead, his writings were taken seriously. The public swallowed Andreae's words as fact, not fiction.

The notion of a secret society with occult knowledge found a receptive audience. The response was intense and immediate. The three publications stirred immense excitement in Europe, each proposing the existence of a brotherhood of alchemists who were preparing to transform the scientific, artistic, and intellectual landscape of the continent. The works were re-issued several times and distributed far and wide. Suddenly, people were declaring themselves Rosicrucians, embracing the ideals of social revolution

"THE PUBLIC SWALLOWED THE SATIRE OF ALCHEMISTS AS FACT, NOT FICTION. THE NOTION OF A SECRET SOCIETY WITH OCCULT KNOWLEDGE STIRRED IMMENSE EXCITEMENT."

through the study of alchemy and mysticism. Many looked to join the Rosicrucian lodges, but did not know where to locate them. Was it all just a hoax?

The truth remains controversial. There is no proof that a Christian Rosenkrantz ever existed. Andreae himself condemned the Rosicrucian Order in his later works *Turris Babel* and

*Mythologia Christiana*, published in 1619. Through his writings, Andreae aimed instead to promote Lutheranism, which is credited as launching the broader Protestant Reformation. As it turned out, many Rosicrucians were also Lutherans. The Rosicrucian movement naturally blended into the larger community of Christian pietism that existed in Germany at

🔲 *Statue of Martin Luther - Founder of Lutheranism*

The Lutheran Seal is a cross inside an open rose, suggesting a link between Lutheranism and the Rosicrucians

the time. At the point when Catholics obtained entry, Andreae rejected the Order altogether. For this reason, many suspect that "C.R." was actually a pseudonym for Sir Francis Bacon. Bacon's unfinished manuscript *The New Atlantis* was published posthumously in 1627. The story curiously describes an earthly, Utopian paradise and a secret brotherhood in which the men wear a "rose cross" on their turbans, heal people without charge, and meet yearly in the temple.

Despite its nebulous origins, the Order continued to grow. No longer under the influence of Andreae, the Rosicrucians splintered into various lodges. Between 1614 and 1620, approximately 400 manuscripts and books were published which discussed the Rose Croix documents. Some endorsed the imaginary brotherhood, while others denounced it. The Rose and Cross symbols became popular. While they are widely known to be emblems associated with mystical systems, the Rosicrucian symbols also conjured other interpretations. Some believe they are linked Andreae's family, whose armorial bearings consisted of St. Andrew's Cross and four roses. Others point to the Lutheran Seal distinguished as well by a cross inside an open rose.

The Rosicrucian constitution of 1763 details the initiation ritual. As it is described, a prospective member is led to a room where certain items are laid out on a table, including: a light, pen, ink, paper, sealing wax, two red

*Sir Francis Bacon*

"MAIER DESCRIBED ALCHEMY NOT AS THE PHYSICAL TRANSFORMATION OF BASE METALS INTO GOLD, BUT RATHER AS A SPIRITUAL PROCESS IN WHICH THE 'BASE' PERSON IS ENLIGHTENED, THEREBY TURNING INTO SPIRITUAL 'GOLD.'"

*Antique brass mortar & pestle*

cords, and a sword. His eyes are then covered, and his hands and neck bound with the cords. A brother then takes him to the door of the lodge, where he knocks nine times. The doorkeeper asks the initiate to state his purpose. "To acquire wisdom, art, and virtue," he responds. "Then live!" the doorkeeper replies. "But your spirit must again rule over your body. You have found grace; arise and be free." At this point, the neophyte is unbound. A wand and a sword are held crosswise for him to lay three fingers upon. He then repeats the oath, promising that

he will keep no secrets from his brethren and will henceforth lead a virtuous life.

As the order spread, Rosicrucianism gained many advocates. German-born Michael Maier emerged as one of its most prominent defenders. A physician and alchemist to Emperor Rudoph II, Maier described alchemy not as the physical transformation of base metals into gold, but rather as a spiritual process in which the "base" person is enlightened, thereby turning into spiritual "gold." He called this path of initiation a "spiritual alchemy." Modern-

day Rosicrucians tend to follow Maier's philosophy, concentrating their work on the soul's development.

The flurry of interest took hold in England as well, attracting Sir Francis Bacon, scientist Robert Boyle, and mathematician John Dee as members. Robert Fludd, a Lutheran minister, published two books with a Rosicrucian bent—*The Compendious Apology for the Fraternity of the Rosy Cross* (1616) and *The Apologetic Tractatus for the Society of the Rosy Cross* (1617). Next came Heydon, an attorney

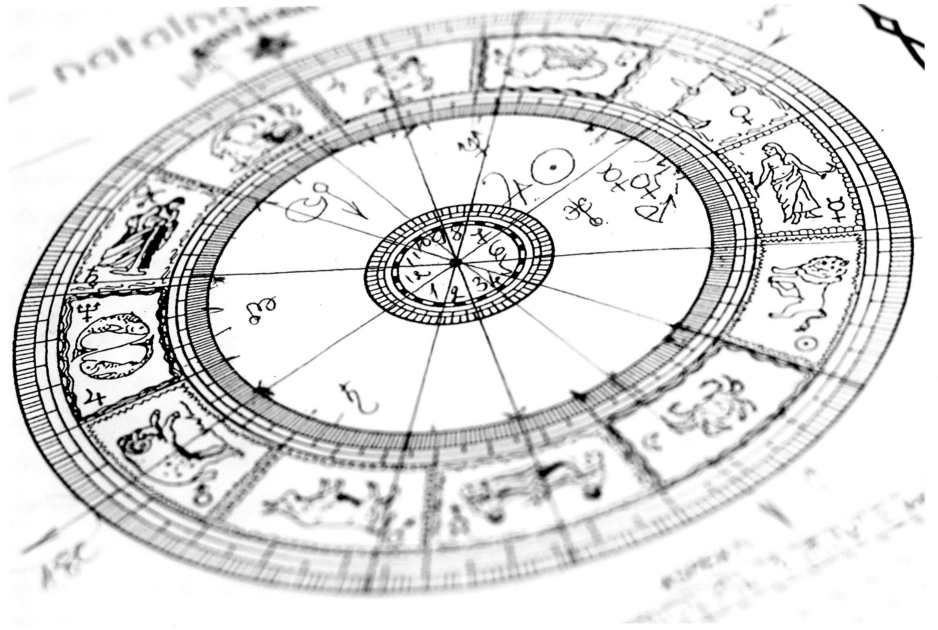

◧ *Horoscope wheel chart*

*A zodiac clock—The rise of Rosicrucianism in the United States inspired the study of astrology*

"EMPEROR JOSEPH II FOUND IT NECESSARY TO CONTROL THE GROUPS BY IMPOSING REGULATIONS. IN 1785, IT WAS DECLARED THAT ALL SECRET SOCIETIES WOULD BE SUPPRESSED. ROSICRUCIANISM PRACTICALLY DISAPPEARED, GRADUALLY FOLDING INTO THE ARMS OF MASONIC LODGES."

who likened the Rosicrucians to Moses and declared them the guardians of sublime secrets. In 1646, the Rosicrucian Society of London was founded by a group of English occultists: Elias Ashmole, William Lilly, Dr. Thomas Warton, Dr. Hewitt and Dr. Pearson. Together they intended to carry out Bacon's uncompleted manuscript, mixing Masonic rituals with the symbolism of alchemists. The lodge steps represented the main ingredients of alchemy—salt, sulfur, and mercury.

Suddenly, the Rosicrucian movement came to a screeching halt. By the 18th century, many secret societies had sprung into existence, among which included the supremely fashionable Freemasonry. Emperor Joseph II found it necessary to control the groups by imposing governmental regulations. In 1785,

it was declared that all societies would be suppressed, except for the Masons, for which the Emperor issued a single patent. Rosicrucianism practically disappeared, gradually folding into the arms of Masonic lodges.

An occult revival in the 19th century reinvigorated Rosicrucianism, which emerged out of Masonry. In 1866, Robert Wentworth Little formed *Societas Rosicruciana in Anglia*, which was only open to Masons and Christians. Freemason William Wynn Wescott became active in the group, increasing its popularity. He later co-founded the ritual magic society Hermetic Order of the Golden Dawn. Around the same time in France, Eliphas Levi wrote three historic volumes on magic: *The Doctrine of Transcendental Magic* (1855), *The Ritual of Transcendental Magic* (1856) and *The History*

*Alchemical signs written on eggs*

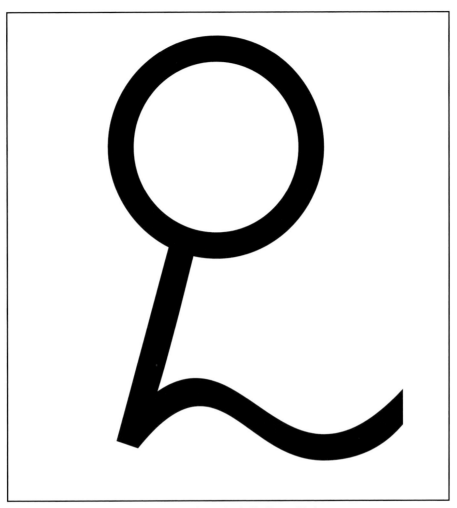

The Alchemical symbol for Quinta Essentia—the Fifth Element after Air, Fire, Water and Earth

of Magic (1860). Levi reportedly welcomed the American Rosicrucian Pascal Beverly Randolph during his trip to France in 1858. At Levi's conclave, Randolph was designated Supreme Master for the Western world. He returned to the United States and established *Fraternitas Rosae Crucis*, the oldest Rosicrucian body in America.

The *Fraternitas Rosae Crucis* enjoyed much success, ultimately ranking number two next to Freemasonry. Freeman B. Dowd succeeded Randolph and expanded the fraternity by establishing temples in Philadelphia, San Francisco, and Denver. After a period of slow growth, Swinburne Clymer rejuvenated the order once again. Taking the helm in 1922, he combined his training in the

occult with his career in non-conventional medicine. His conflicts with the American Medical Association found reprieve inside the Order. He set up headquarters in Pennsylvania and launched the Philosophical Publishing Company, through which he published his own writings and reissued many of Rudolph's works. He also built a healing complex, equipped with a chiropractic office and a clinic specializing in natural healing methods. The group still exists, offering mail-order instruction based on the teachings of spiritual alchemy.

Rudolph did much to enhance the image of Rosicrucians, but he was never able to overcome the splinter effect inherent from the start. Today many organizations claim to be descendants of the Order—an estimated eight

groups in the United States alone. Each one accepts the name Rosicrucian and a version of the legend as part of its history.

Several Rosicrucian groups trace their lineage to Theosophical Society—the largest one being The Rosicrucian Fellowship, founded by Max Heindel in 1907. Heindel was an engineer who studied theosophy in Germany. Upon returning to America, he published *The Rosicrucian Cosmo-Conception*, which comprises the basic teachings of the fellowship. It is a largely Christian organization that has closer ties to theosophy and astrology than original Rosicrucian thought. It is thought that Heindel's writings prompted the study of astrology in the United States. He established his first center in Columbus, Ohio, and then

*San Jose, California is the headquarters for AMORC, the most famous modern-day Rosicrucian group*

# "THE VARIOUS SOCIETIES OF THE ROSE CROSS ALL CLAIM TO PRESERVE ANCIENT WISDOM AND VALUE THE INNER SANCTUM OF SECRECY."

went on to create many more along the coast of California. Today the society is headquartered on Mt. Ecclesia in Oceanside and offers courses in astrology and the occult. The organization claims that its secret brotherhood is still active and working for the benefit of humanity. It also prides itself on being highly selective, accepting only those who are spiritually "evolved" into its inner branch of the Rosicrucian movement.

The most famous modern-day group is The Ancient and Mystical Order Rosae Crucis, otherwise known as AMORC. It was formed in 1915 by Harvey Spencer Lewis, a writer and occultist living in New York City. He started the group after visiting France, where he was initiated and authorized to start an organization in America. The first convention was held in 1917, and a year later, the Order moved its headquarters to San Francisco. Soon after, Lewis incorporated the Pristine Church of the Rose Cross, an affiliated religious order. However, the church only lasted a few years, as AMORC sought to emphasize fellowship over religion. Today the organization is headquartered in San Jose, California. The complex includes the Rose-Croix University, a Planetarium and the Rosicrucian Research Library, all of which attract the curiosity of tourists. AMORC describes itself as "a school of practical mysticism, which encourages you

to be open-minded, questioning, and to test the value of the principles you are learning by actively using them in your daily life." Like Fraternitas Rosae Crucis, the organization offers mail-order instruction for members, which is referred to as "a school of practical mysticism" that offers a "gradual development of your natural psychic and spiritual abilities." The web site offers a wealth of information about the society's origins, philosophy and format of the weekly teachings. Membership also includes a subscription to the monthly magazine *The Rosicrucian Forum*, while *The Rosicrucian Digest* is available to non-members.

The various societies of the Rose Cross may differ significantly from the original Rosicrucian teachings, yet they all claim to preserve ancient wisdom and value the inner sanctum of secrecy. Above all, each one argues that its teachings are relevant and essential. "In the 21st century, we feel strongly that these teachings will play an increasing role in humanity's evolution," says AMORC on its website. "With fast-paced technological advancement and its effects upon the environment and the human psyche, people are searching for an inner, ever-reliable source of strength and balance."

Whether or not Christian Rosenkrantz was real or a hoax, the Rosicrucian legend has spawned a mystical belief system that is still attracting followers today.

*1920s mafiosos*

# CHAPTER 4:

# MAFIA
# (COSA NOSTRA)

BEGINNING IN THE 1600S, "LA COSA NOSTRA"
CAME INTO BEING AS A REACTION TO FOREIGN
INVASION AND A NEED FOR SELF-DEFENSE.

In 1990, the FBI recorded an induction
ritual admitting Robert "Bobby Dee"
Deluca into Boston's Patriarca family, one
of the most prominent Mafia families outside
New York.

"I, Robert Deluca, want to enter this
organization to protect my family and to protect
my friends. I swear not to divulge this secret
and to obey, with love and *omertà*." Each man
then pricked his index finger and dropped his
blood on to a holy card bearing an image of the
Patriarca family saint. The card was set afire,
and Deluca repeated the second oath: "As burns
the saint, so will burn my soul. I enter alive into
this organization and leave it dead."

*The Mafia originated on the island of Sicily, off the coast of Italy*

*Omertà* is "the code of silence" sealed in a Mafia initiation ceremony. Within the organization's rules and conduct, breaking the oath of omertà is punishable by death. Even if a Mafia member is condemned for a crime he has not committed, he is required to serve the sentence without giving authorities any information about the real criminal. Membership is for life. There is no retirement from the Mafia—unless you are prepared to die.

Also known as "La Cosa Nostra," the Mafia first originated in Sicily in reaction to its long history of foreign invasion. By the 1600s, the Spanish rulers had imposed censorship and a fear of torture upon anyone who defied its authority. The Sicilians did not believe in effective government and law enforcement,

and thus, formed their own protection society. The English translation of "La Cosa Nostra" is "this thing of ours," a reflection of the Sicilians' instinct to defend their own. Bandit gangs started to appear, targeting feudal lords. Gradually, the lords retreated to Palermo, leaving management of their properties to locally respected *gabelloti*. These men would collect taxes, accompanied by associates called *campieri*. This early system and structure served as the foundation for what would emerge as the biggest organized crime phenomenon in the world.

Eventually, four Mafia groups took hold in Italy: the Sicilian Mafia in Palermo, 'Ndrangheta in Calabria, Sacra Corona Unita in Apuila, and Camorra in Naples. The

*A map of Palermo*

Sicilian Mafia is the most powerful, with 5,000 members divided among 186 families, 67 of which are located in Palermo. The hierarchy within families follows a classic pyramidal structure:

### Capo Crimini / Capo de tutti capi (Boss):

The head of the family, usually reigning as a dictator, sometimes called the don or "godfather." The Boss receives a cut of every operation taken on by every member of his family.

### Capo Bastone (Underboss):

The second-in-command of the family, usually appointed by the Boss. The Underboss is controlled by the Boss and in charge of all of the Capos. He is usually first in line to become Acting Boss if the Boss is imprisoned or dies.

### Consigliere:

An advisor to the family. This person is often a low-profile gangster who can be trusted. They are used as a mediator of disputes or as a representative or aide in meetings with other families.

### Caporegime (Capo):

A Capo is in charge of a crew. There are usually four to six crews in each family, each one consisting of up to ten Soldiers.

### Sgarrista (Soldiers):

Members of the family, who carry out the family's daily business. Soldiers start as Associates that have proven themselves. A Capo may recommend an up-and-coming Associate to be a new member.

### Piciotto (Associate):

A low-ranking soldier who is not a member of the mob. An Associate's role is similar to that of an errand boy.

Benito Mussolini rose to power in the 1920s and cracked down on the Italian Mafia

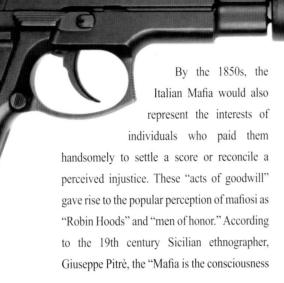

*9mm gun with silencer*

By the 1850s, the Italian Mafia would also represent the interests of individuals who paid them handsomely to settle a score or reconcile a perceived injustice. These "acts of goodwill" gave rise to the popular perception of mafiosi as "Robin Hoods" and "men of honor." According to the 19th century Sicilian ethnographer, Giuseppe Pitrè, the "Mafia is the consciousness of one's own worth, the exaggerated concept of individual force as the sole arbiter of every conflict, of every clash of interests or ideas." However, the Mafia's dominating influence experienced a significant backlash when Benito Mussolini and his fascist dictatorship rose to power in the 1920s. Mussolini enlisted the help of Cesar Mori to crack down on the Italian Mafia, essentially shutting down their operations by brutal force. Many Italian mafiosos fled the country, largely to Brazil and the United States.

The first mafia-based crime in the U.S. occurred in New Orleans. In 1890, the Sicilian crime family murdered the local chief of police, David Hennessy, who had been investigating them. Despite the overwhelming evidence against them, the culprits were acquitted. The decision spurred great controversy, and the following month a lynch mob stormed the jail,

*Marijuana and money*

*Above: A beer truck. The Mafia took off in America during the Prohibition in the 1920s*

# "THE OUTLAWING OF ALCOHOL IN THE UNITED STATES CREATED A HIGH-PROFIT OPPORTUNITY FOR CRIMINALS"

*New Orleans was the site of the first Mafia crime in the United States*

hanging 11 of the 17 members still waiting to be brought to trial. Suffice it to say, the Mafia did not stick around New Orleans for long, eventually spreading to other American cities including New York, Chicago, Cleveland, and Detroit. Between 1890 and 1920, the Black Hand gangs set up operations in Italian immigrant communties and ran extortion rackets. Black Hand gangsters would threaten local merchants by mail if their extortion demands were not met. They were known to "decorate" the threats with a hand covered in black ink at the bottom of the page.

The Prohibition of 1919 presented an ideal environment for the Mafia to take hold in America. The outlawing of alcohol in the United States created a high-profit opportunity for criminals. People still wanted their liquor, and since it was no longer available legally, a ripe situation presented itself for criminals to satisfy the demand. "It's all a matter of supply and demand," says Matt Heron, the chief of the FBI's New York organized crime unit. "There's a demand for what they have to offer, and as long as that's there, they'll find a way to supply it." The Mafia set about distributing products below the radar of law enforcement. By the time Prohibition was repealed in 1933, the organization was firmly intact and soon turned to other businesses such as gambling, narcotics, prostitution, and protection rackets.

The Five Families dominated organized crime in New York City

Lucky Luciano created the framework of the American Mafia as it exists today

By the late 1920s and early 1930s, a fierce competition was brewing in New York among rival crime families vying for control. It was called the "Castellammarese War"—a bloody struggle between Joe Masseria and Salvatore Maranzano, the heads of two warring factions. Sicilian Mafioso Lucky Luciano took control by eliminating both men in order to create a new structure for Cosa Nostra. Luciano had trained in the Five Points gang under John Torrio, and by 1925, controlled all of the prostitution business in Manhattan. In 1931 he organized the New York Mafia into Five Families, and established the Commission, its governing body. Under Luciano's leadership, the 26 crime families in America aligned themselves under

the National Crime Syndicate, am umbrella organization comprised of a national board of directors that ruled the American underworld. Historians credit Luciano with creating the framework of the Mafia, as it still exists today.

The formation of the Commission did not stop the gang wars, but it did diminish their power and help keep them out of the public eye. Its primary purpose was to oversee all the Mafia activities and mediate disputes between families. While there was no "Super Boss," the savvy Luciano made himself its Chairman. He also appointed Meyer Lansky, the preeminent Jewish gangster in New York, to the role of Chief Advisor. In addition to the five New York family bosses, the Commission included Buffalo boss Stefano Magaddino and Chicago boss "Scarface" Al Capone. Like Luciano, Capone had graduated from the Five Points gang. Torrio then invited him to Chicago, where in 1925, he bequeathed to Capone his $50 million empire.

While Capone ruled Chicago, the Five Families dominated organized crime in New York. They acquired their names after prominent early members: the Bonanno family, the Colombo family, the Gambino family, the Genovese family, and the Lucchese family. Each one has a legendary story of its own to tell.

*Mafioso Al Capone domineered over Chicago*

"MEANWHILE, A MAN CALLING HIMSELF DONNIE BRASCO HAD BEEN INVITED TO BECOME A FULL MEMBER OF THE FAMILY. 'BRASCO' WAS ACTUALLY AN UNDERCOVER COP FOR THE FBI, JOE PISTONE, WHO HAD INFILTRATED THE ORGANIZATION."

## The Bonnano Family

At 26 years old of age, Joseph "Joe Bananas" Bonnano was the youngest boss of the Five Families. He directed the family into organized crime ventures such as gambling, loan-sharking, and racketeering. The Bonnano family was considered the most close-knit, because it comprised mostly Sicilians from the seaside town where Bonnano was born—Casellamare del Golfo. However, many family members were becoming frustrated with Bonnano, complaining that he was never around. The Commission eventually replaced him with *caporegime* Gaspar DiGregorio, and thereby instigated what is known as "The Bonnano War."

Skirmishes took place as members divided their loyalties between Bonnano and DeGregorio. Again, the Commission grew tired of the infighting and replaced DeGregorio with Paul Sciacca. Both factions aligned themselves under Sciacca, but by that time, the family had lost its seat on the Commission. Philip "Rusty" Rastelli eventually took the throne. The internal strife continued, as rumors spread of an overthrow. Rastelli promptly had three traitorous men eliminated. Meanwhile, a man calling himself Donnie Brasco had been invited to become a full member of the family. "Brasco" was actually an undercover cop for the FBI, Joe Pistone, who had infiltrated the organization in the 1970s. Pistone's testimony delivered justice for the murders and sent Rastelli and his hitman to prison. This case, now referred to as "Donnie Brasco," was the first ever penetration of an organized crime family by the FBI. The story was turned into a 1997 film by the same name, starring Johnny Depp and Al Pacino.

For a period Rastelli ruled the family from prison, and then in 1991, he gave way to the promotion of Joseph Massino. Massino helped the Bonnano family re-emerge to the top of New York's crime families. He concentrated on narcotics trade and other businesses that would draw less attention from the authorities, including loan sharking and money laundering. He also helped the family secure a seat on the Commission once again.

In more recent years, several high-level defections and convictions have caused the family to lose power, now a shell of its former self. In 2004 Massino became the first serving boss to turn informant in order to spare himself the death penalty.

*Three Bad Boys (1919)*

*Brooklyn Bridge / The Colombo crime family was based in Brooklyn*

> "FAMILY MEMBERS BEGAN MAKING DEALS FOR THEMSELVES BY COOPERATING WITH LAW ENFORCEMENT. THE MOBSTERS BEGAN TURNING ON EACH OTHER, GIVING AUTHORITIES THE OPPORTUNITY TO EXPLOIT THE SITUATION AND CRACK DOWN ON ORGANIZED CRIME."

## The Colombo family

This Brooklyn-based family was first led by Joe Profaci, a man hated by his underlings. Profaci taxed his men heavily and treated them brutally if they did not comply. Surprisingly, his authority was not seriously challenged. He lived a life of luxury, primarily acquiring his wealth through the traditional Mafia enterprises of extortion and protection rackets. Profaci's death in 1962 eventually gave rise to Joseph "Joe C" Colombo as the new boss. The family had entered a new era. It rechristened itself as "Colombo" as a way to purge its former association with the despised Profaci.

As an activist for Italian-Americans, Colombo set up the Italian-American Civil Rights League to defend against prejudice within the legal system. Through his involvement in the League, he was frequently seen in public and in the press at a time when most Mafia bosses were only seen defending themselves in court. Colombo reached his end at a rally in 1971 where he was gunned down by a lone shooter, Jerome Johnson. Some say that it may have been set up by rogue law enforcement. He survived, comatose, until his death in 1977.

Carmine Persico had emerged as the next likely boss, but was currently behind bars. He nonetheless ran the family from prison, with Gennaro "Jerry Lang" Langella as his street boss. Ultimately, their rule came to an end when they both received a 100-year sentence during a 1987 RICO trial. The one single event that did more than anything to curb organized crime was the passage of the RICO statutes in 1970. Officially known as "The Racketeer Influenced and Corrupt Organizations Act," this United States federal law permits the prosecution of a person or group for a racketeering charge, provided that they have committed any two of 35 crimes within a 10-year period. In the past, a conviction for loan sharking or extortion might carry a three-year sentence, whereas now under RICO, prosecutors can lump several crimes under a single racketeering statute. "What happens then, when you start prosecuting folks," says FBI chief Heron, "that 3-5 year sentence becomes 25 years. With multiple counts, it's 100 years in prison." As a result, family members began making deals for themselves by cooperating with law enforcement. The mobsters began turning on each other, giving authorities the opportunity to exploit the situation and crack down on organized crime.

Today Persico allegedly remains the head of the diluted Colombo family while residing in a penitentiary in North Carolina. His son, Alphonse "Allie" Persico, was earmarked to take over but is currently on trial for murder. He could face a lifetime in prison if convicted.

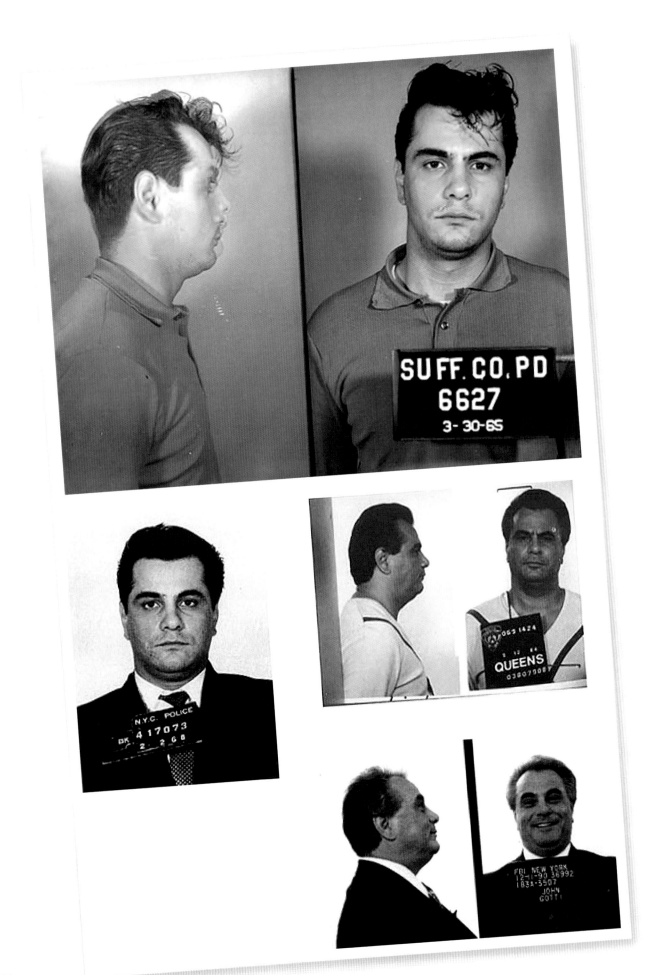

## The Gambino family

Under the leadership of Carlo Gambino, the Gambino family became one of the most powerful families in the National Crime Syndicate. During his 20-year reign (1956-1976), Gambino built the family into a financial powerhouse primarily through gambling and narcotics. Upon his death, Paul "Big Paulie" Castellano took over.

The FBI had targeted the Gambinos as the easiest family to infiltrate. They bugged Castellano's home and caught him negotiating illegal deals. By the early 1980s, Big Paulie had numerous charges against his name and was facing conviction in the Mafia Commission Trial. In that landmark case (1985-1986), United States Attorney Rudolph Giuliani indicted 11 organized crime figures, including the heads of New York's Five Families, under the RICO Act. The charges that included extortion, labor racketeering, and murder for hire. The case struck a blow against the Commission. While out on bail, Castellano and an associate were shot dead outside Sparks Steak House in Manhattan on the orders of John Gotti.

Gotti took the helm. Known as the "Dapper Don," Gotti was famous for his $10,000 hand-tailored suits and silk ties, as well as his outspoken personality that catered to the media. He became the poster child of all mobsters. His flamboyance manifested itself in the free and lavish parties he threw in his Queens neighborhood. His annual Fourth of July celebration featured an elaborate fireworks display and became a major media event. He preferred holding meetings while walking in public to avoid being wiretapped. Eventually, he earned the nickname "Teflon Don" due to his series of acquittals. Finally, one of his underlings, Sammy "The Bull" Gravano,

*John Gotti, also known as the 'Dapper Don', ruled the Gambino crime family 1985-2002*

reversed his fortunes when he testified against Gotti. In 1992, Gotti was convicted and received a life sentence without parole.

Gotti nonetheless continued to rule the family from prison, assigning the day-to-day operations to capos John "Jackie Nose" D'Amico and Nick Corozzo. Allegedly Gotti's son, John Jr., took on the role of boss between 1992-1999, but did not have the ruthlessness that his father embodied. In 1999, John Jr. was charged with racketeering and sentenced to six years behind bars. He claimed in court that he had retired from the Mafia, and upon his release, that he wanted to take his family

to Canada. Upon Gotti Sr.'s death in 2002, the reins thus passed to his brother, Peter.

## The Genovese family

Under Frank Costello's leadership, the Genovese family began its reputation as the most powerful, secretive, and disciplined of the Five Families. Costello became known as the "Prime Minister" of the underworld. He was well connected to law enforcement, judges, and politicians. It is said that during his reign as mob boss, no judge in New York was appointed

without his consent. Costello was also known for throwing parties, whose guests included FBI director J. Edgar Hoover.

Starting in 1950, federal investigations began to penetrate the underworld. The Kefauver Committee hearings (1950-1951) exposed the bosses and criminal operations to the media and public. Costello agreed to testify and became the highlight of this event. His only condition was that his face would not be shown- only his hands. Led by Senator Estes Kefauver, the hearings were covered by the three major networks and held all of America's attention. It forced Hoover to admit that the underworld

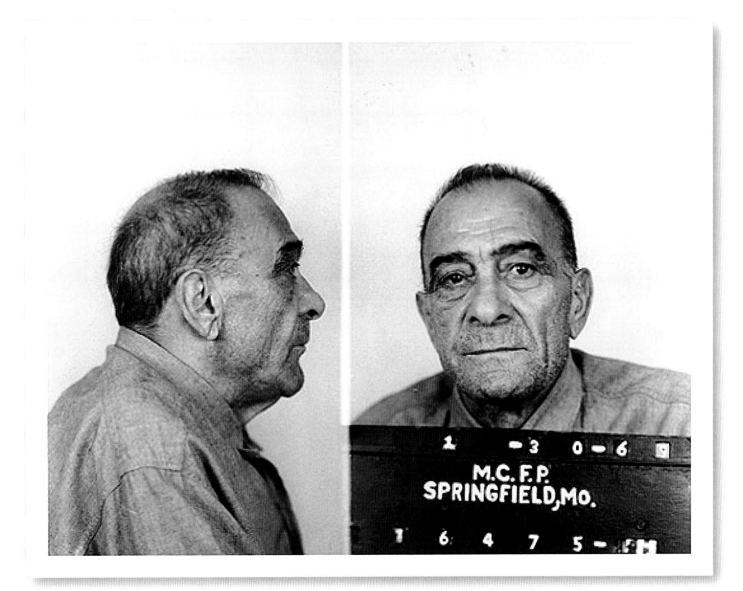

*Vito Genovese was the Boss of the Genovese crime family 1957-1969*

 *J. Edgar Hoover, the first director of the Federal Bureau Investigation (FBI), held office from 1935 until his death in 1972*

of organized crime existed, a fact that both he and the FBI had long denied and ignored. Costello's refusal to answer all the questions and eventual walkout catapulted him to the status of America's #1 Gangster. Behind the scenes, the family grumbled about Costello's poor performance. In 1957, Vito Genovese and gunman Vincent "Chin" Gigante made an attempt to kill off Costello in the lobby of his Manhattan apartment building, but botched the hit. Afterwards, Costello decided almost immediately to retire from his position as Boss, and passed the baton to his friend

and ally Albert Anastasia. In little time, Anastasia was taken out in the barbershop of Manhattan's Sheraton hotel, as he was getting a haircut.

Genovese finally secured his position as Boss. In 1957, he called a national meeting gathering the heads of all the families for a strategy session. They met at the Apalachin, the New York estate of Northeastern family boss Joseph "The Barber" Barbara. However, New York state troopers discovered the "secret" meeting. The delegates representing the 26 American Mafia families tried to flee, but over

 *Rudolph "Rudy" Guiliani indicted 11 organized crime leaders during the Mafia Commission Trial in 1985-1986*

60 were detained and later indicted. It is a famous story in the history of organized crime. The Apalachin Meeting finally confirmed the existence of the National Crime Syndicate. Genovese later received a 15-year sentence for drug trafficking, yet still ran the family behind bars. Many bosses placed blame on Genovese and would never forgive him. He died in an Atlanta prison in 1969.

The baton then passed from Vincent "Chin" Gigante to Dominick "Quiet Dom" Cirillo, who served effectively as "street boss" for several years. He earned his nickname due to his laid-back, reserved manner. He was known to conduct his business in private, by shunning telephones and opting for less flashy cars. Then, in 2005, Cirillo pled guilty on charges of racketeering, and the following year was sentenced to 46 months in prison. Regardless, the Genovese Family is still arguably the richest and most powerful family in the country. The current Genovese boss is Mario Gigante, the older brother of "Chin."

## The Lucchese family

Gaetano "Tommy" Gagliano trained his underboss Gaetano "Tommy" Lucchese to treat their family members well, while they profited in the trucking and clothing industries. When Lucchese took over, he carried on these traditions and established the family as one of the most profitable in New York. He furthered the family's interests by controlling the Teamsters' unions and developing close relationships with politicians and judiciary members. He did all of this while maintaining a low profile, which earned him great respect in the Mafia community. Lucchese managed to avoid any convictions during his 44 years in the world of organized crime.

The J Edgar Hoover Building, the headquarters for the FBI

Old police box for emergencies

The Lucchese family is responsible for the infamous French Connection scheme, which distributed heroin worth millions of dollars up and down the East Coast during the early 1970s. It is suspected that the smuggling operation involved corrupt NYPD officers who allowed the drugs to be stored on police property. The bust was made when authorities noticed insects eating the storage bags. By that time, the "heroin" had been replaced with bags of baking flour. The then-current Lucchese boss Carmine "Gribbs" Tramunti was eventually convicted in 1974.

The power transferred to Anthony "Tony Ducks" Corallo, who continued to work closely with the trade unions as well as Jimmy Hoffa, the international president of the Teamsters' Union (who later disappeared). The authorities kept a close eye on Corallo, still trafficking narcotics. They managed to plant a bug in Corallo's car, which secured

" IN 1990 THE BOSS AND UNDERBOSS OF THE LUCCHESE FAMILY WENT INTO HIDING AND RULED THE FAMILY FROM AFAR. THEY ORDERED THE EXECUTION OF ANYONE THEY DEEMED TROUBLESOME, CAUSING FAMILY MEMBERS TO TURN INFORMANT TO SAVE THEIR OWN LIVES. "

evidence sufficient to send Corallo to prison for life following a RICO trial. When he decided to step down as Boss, he handpicked his successors: Vittorio "Vic" Amuso as Boss, and Anthony Casso as Underboss.

The following period was one of the most turbulent the Lucchese family has ever seen. Amuso and Casso were both indicted in a racketeering investigation. In 1990 they went into hiding and ruled the family from afar. They ordered the execution of anyone they deemed troublesome, causing family members to turn informant to save their own lives. The FBI soon captured both Amuso and Casso. Casso immediately struck a witness deal, but Amuso refused to turn. When Alphonse "Little Al" D'Arco, acting Boss at the time, decided to cooperate with the authorities, many others followed suit and testified against Amuso. The loss of faith in the former bosses had a devastating effect on the family.

Amuso is currently serving a life sentence at a federal penitentiary in Kentucky. He is still considered the official boss, but it is hard to imagine how effective he is from his prison cell.

The American Mafia has suffered greatly from turncoats, federal prosecution, and internal conflicts due to bad leadership. It seems there is no longer a code of silence among the toughest of Mafiosos. Since the 1970s, authorities have proven particularly effective in persuading flip soldiers to break the *omertà* and betray their bosses. Joe Valachi was the first member to go on record as an informant. In 1963, he testified before U.S. Senate McClellan Committee about the Mafia's presence. A low-ranking soldier in the Genovese family, Valachi used the term *"Cosa Nostra"* for the first time, making it a household name. Although his disclosures never led directly to the prosecution of family leaders, he provided many details about the Mafia's history and operations. The effect was devastating to the mob, which was still

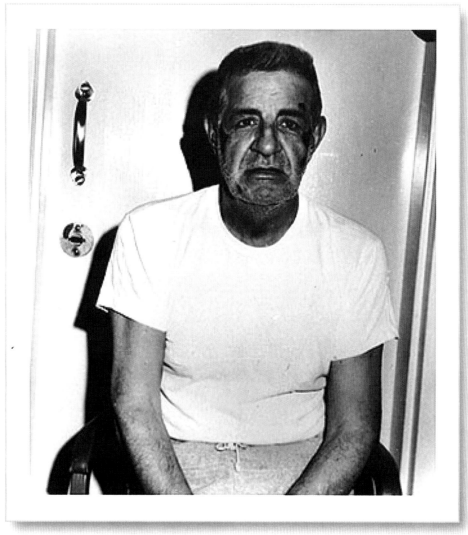

*▣ Joe Valachi was the first Mafia member to go on record as an informant*

reeling from the Apalachin Meeting. Valachi's motivations are still subject to debate. He claimed to be testifying against an organization that ruined his life, but it is also possible that he was looking to the government to spare him from the death penalty for a murder charge.

It was a Sicilian Mafioso, Tommy Buscetta, who first described the initiation ritual to authorities. Although Buscetta was not the first *pentito* (informant) in the Italian witness protection program, he is widely recognized as the first important one to break *omertà*. Buscetta had become disillusioned

with the Mafia, and subsequently decided to help Anti-mafia judges Giovanni Falcone and Paolo Borsellino to fight organized crime (both judges were later killed by the Mafia). Buscetta's testimony in the New York Pizza Connection Trial led to the conviction of many Italian and American mobsters. He also became the star witness of the Maxi Trial, which took place in Sicily in the mid-1980s and sent almost 350 members to prison. As a reward for his assistance, Buscetta was permitted to live peacefully in the USA under a new identity until his death in 2000 of cancer.

Today American crime families are reaching across the globe to Sicily to recruit new members. There, they say, they are sure to find honorable men to uphold the principles of the "real" Mafia. They are looking for men who are willing to die before breaking the *omertà* code of silence. It's not clear if these Sicilian recruits have assumed leadership roles in the American families, but they are establishing themselves and may become more powerful in the foreseeable future.

So what is the status of the Mafia today? Statistics show that the Italian Mafia groups

The American Mafia is returning to the streets of Sicily to recruit new members

Although often glamorized in the media, the "real" Mafia remain secretive

*The Italian flag*

are still going strong. A report by the Eurispes Research Institute produced the following report in 2003:

• In the previous four years, Italy's Mafia groups earned 32 billion euros (approx. US $42.5 billion) and murdered approximately 700 people.

• 18 billion euros (approx. US $24 billion) earned from drug trafficking; 7 billion euros (approx. US $9 billion) went to Ndrangheta Mafia; 5 billion euros (approx. US $6.5 billion) for the Camorra gang.

• Of 666 murders recorded between 1999 and 2003, half were linked to Camorra.

Meanwhile, the portrayals in the American media continue to glamorize these criminals and turn them into celebrities. Films like *The Godfather* and the television series *The Sopranos* have humanized them. "There's a tendency in movies and the press to shine a sympathetic light on these guys," says Matt Heron of the FBI, "but you have to remember who they are, and what they represent."

In reality, it seems that the American Mafia is a shell of what it used to be. Still, although they may be wounded, they are not dead. Most likely, they will never die. Where there continues to be a demand, they will supply.

>—i—◆>—O—<◆—i—<

CHAPTER 5:

# FREEMASONS

A FAVORITE OF THE CONSPIRACY BUFFS, THE
INFLUENCE OF FREEMASONRY REACHES FROM
MEDIEVAL LONDON TO THE FOUNDERS OF THE
UNITED STATES OF AMERICA

When the term "secret society" is mentioned, the first thing that usually comes to mind is the Freemasons. How can that be possible when their telephone numbers and meeting locations are publicly listed in directories, not to mention that each year the organization gives away millions of dollars to charity? As Benjamin Franklin once said, "The great secret of Freemasonry is that there is no secret at all."

Those who look deeper will discover that the Freemasons lurk behind every treaty, battle, and statute in American history. They have held more offices and dominated more seats in American government than any organization. Did you know that 13 of the 19 signers of the U.S. Constitution were Freemasons, as well as 9 of the 59 signers of the Declaration of Independence? For this reason, many believe that the Freemasons instigated the American Revolution. In fact, this fraternal society and the Founding Fathers held many ideals in common: honorable civic-mindedness, a high regard for learning and progress, and religious tolerance. According to Masonic websites, 14 Presidents of the United States have been Masons, including George Washington, Andrew Jackson, and Franklin Roosevelt. Two Presidents, Gerald Ford and Harry Truman, reached the 33rd degree status, the highest level of Freemasonry.

It is this remarkable aggregate of power that begs suspicion about the society's true purpose. The conspiracy buffs will tell you that the Freemasons have had their hands in every aspect of American culture, including its currency. Just take a look at the back of the U.S.

*Great Seal from the U.S. One Dollar bill*

A Revolutionary War cannon. Freemasonry became popular after the American Revolution, boasting over 100 lodges by 1776

*The United States Constitution—13 of the 19 signers were Freemasons*

dollar bill, emblazoned with the same floating eye and pyramid that appears on the Masonic Seal. Or notice the street plan of Washington DC, designed in the form of an "evil" pentagram by Masonic architect Pierre Charles L'Enfant. Each example, they say, gives further credence to the society's intention to overthrow the United States government, undermine Catholicism, and take over the world.

Yet those who look again might uncover a different story. In 1821 Thomas Smith Webb argued that the Masons adopted their symbols in 1787, 14 years after the Great American Seal was created. By the same token, city-street planning is often in the form of geometric shapes. Who ever said pentagrams are "evil," anyway? A true student of Freemasonry discovers that the actual Masonic tenets are quite different than the rumored interpretations. Members maintain that their true motive is, and always has been, to make a man a better man, plain and simple. They emphasize tradition, morality, self-improvement and fraternity, which are reflected in the oath taken: "You agree to be a good man and true; you agree to conform to the laws of the country in which you reside; you promise not to be concerned with plots and conspiracies of the government." Hardly threatening. But, what about the secret codes, hidden treasures, and plots to take over the world?

President Harry S. Truman achieved the 33rd status, the highest level in Masonry

Secrecy is in fact part of the Freemason's origin. Dating all the way back to 17th-century England, the fraternal order descended from medieval guilds of stonemasons and cathedral builders. References to the Masons date as early as 1390, but they did not become official until 1717, when four London lodges united to establish the United Grand Lodge of England. These tradesmen, who laid the cornerstones of important government buildings and churches, came together to protect their skills and talents. New initiates were sworn to silence about the secrets of their craft to ensure those in the guild

continued success. Wearing their distinctive aprons, the members of "the craft," as Masonry is called, formed community-based lodges each with a master leader. The three degrees of the craft are listed as: 1) Entered Apprentice, 2) Fellow Craft, and 3) Master Mason. The moral lessons of Masonry are communicated through allegorical ritual, as the candidate passes through these degrees.

From its early days, the society welcomed selected patrons into their ranks, who pledged their loyalties in kind. They were drawn to the masonry's ties to ancient architecture,

geometry and other rational arts and sciences. Based on this historic tradition, the principle symbols of masonry feature a compass with the letter "G" in a square, standing for "geometry." The fraternal group gradually moved from a practical guild to a more philosophical association of businessmen, absorbing members of intellect from Britain's scientific Royal Society. They explored and discussed the laws of nature, and followed the development of modern experimental science. In their studies of ancient civilizations, the Temple of Solomon also became deeply embedded in Masonic lore.

Y (WHO) SE... 
...MS OF GOV...NMENT BASED ON
...REGIMENTATION OF ALL HUMAN
...S BY A HANDFUL OF INDIVIDUAL
...ERS... CALL THIS A NEW ORDER.
...NOT NEW AND IT IS NOT ORDER.

Statue of Franklin D. Roosevelt, one of 14 American Presidents who have been Freemasons

*Compass and square, the symbols of Masonry*

Over time, the order cultivated a bridge between the gentlemanly class of businessmen and the artisans who aspired to that establishment. Freemasonry encouraged social movement and a more inclusive elite—a reputation that has endured over time.

The Masons embraced ideas of the Enlightenment, championing not only freedoms of thought, but also spirituality. While some called it a pseudo-religion, the Freemasons have always been non-denominational, asking that members simply recognize a Supreme Being. In Masonic ritual, this Supreme Being is referred to as the Great Architect of the Universe or Grand Geometer, leaving room for all religions to join. This broad tolerance provoked condemnation by the Roman Catholic Church, which deemed the order anti-Christian. In 1738, Pope Clement XII forbade Catholics to be members and directed the "Inquisitors of Heretical Depravity" to take action against those who became Masons or assisted Freemasonry in any way. He ordered excommunication as punishment for any transgressions. A few years later, Pope Benedict XIV declared six dangers associated with Masonry: 1) their interfaith practices, 2) their secrecy, 3) their oath, 4) their opposition to church and state, 5) the interdiction of Freemasonry in various countries, and 6) their immorality.

By the mid-1700s the order had crossed the Atlantic, establishing the American Lodge of Boston in 1733. It was at the Bunch of Grapes Tavern where fellow Masons—Paul Revere, George Washington, and John Hancock—would gather to discuss politics and plan action. After the American Revolution, the fraternal organization became very powerful, boasting over 100 lodges by 1776. At that point, the American Freemasons broke ties with the London Grand Lodges and reorganized under state lodges, while also moving into

"THE MASONS EMBRACED IDEAS OF THE ENLIGHTENMENT, CHAMPIONING NOT ONLY FREEDOMS OF THOUGHT, BUT ALSO SPIRITUALITY."

the country's interior towards the ever-advancing frontier. Due to widespread racism and segregation at the time, a group of black Americans formed Prince Hall Freemasonry. Overall membership jumped from 16,000 in 1800 to about 80,000 in 1822, the equivalent to approximately 5 per cent of the nation's eligible male population. A visit by Lafayette, a fellow Mason, further infused the order with an aura of prestige during his tour of the United States in 1824 and 1825.

The emphasis on mystical rituals and oaths of secrecy, meanwhile, fostered mistrust among outsiders. Between 1790 and 1820 the American

Masons had imported two new higher-degree systems from Europe—the York rites from England, and the Scottish rites from France. The Master Mason degree thus expanded its instruction to 33 degrees. While the elaborate rites associated with these traditions attracted new members, they also aroused suspicions. After all, the skeptics murmured, anything so secret must be satanic and subversive. As the order's influence expanded, people began to speculate about its true motives and accused the masons of being elitist. The fraternal society also behaved in mysterious ways that only encouraged these feelings. For instance, the

Scottish Rite Freemasonry was established in Charleston, South Carolina precisely because it was aligned with the 33rd parallel.

The death of William Morgan in 1826 justified all these floating suspicions. Morgan had been blacklisted by a New York lodge, and claimed to be writing a book that attacked Freemasonry, threatening to reveal all the Masons' deep, dark secrets. Suddenly, Morgan vanished and his printer's shop was burned to the ground. Word spread that the Masons had gotten away with murder, spurring fierce anti-Masonic sentiment. The short-lived Anti-Masonic Party, founded in 1830, nearly drove

*Masonic Lodge in San Juan Bautista, California*

🔲 *Masonic Compass and the letter 'G'*

the fraternity out of existence. While New York State had been home to about 500 local lodges in the mid 1820's, only 26 lodges sent representatives to the statewide meeting in 1837. Almost two-thirds of Indiana's lodges had shut down by the same year. By the end of the 1830's the Masons had begun to make a comeback but would never again enjoy the same supreme respect and esteem.

The Freemasons, above all, are a story about reinvention. And sure enough, after the Civil War and into the 1870s, the Masons reemerged as a model for more than 300 fraternal groups that appeared during the next 50 years. Their renewed image came in the form of charitable works, including the support of schools and hospitals, a blending of fraternity with philanthropy. Those Masons who completed a high level of Masonry were eligible to join the Nobles of the Mystic Shrine, first established in 1870. A particularly jovial group of Masons, the Shriners stressed fun and fellowship more than ritual, reflective of an age that was coming to value personality over ideals of honor and character. This allied group has since evolved to an impressive charity organization, boasting a 2006 budget of US $649 million for Shriners' Hospitals.

From there, Masonic membership continued to multiply, reaching its peak of four million in the 1950s and 1960s. From those glory days, the fraternity has experienced a steady decline. Today's membership maintains a respectable two million at large, with an average age of 60 plus. The group only admits men, but has opened associated women's orders, including Order of the Eastern Star and the Order of the Amaranth. Prince Hall has grown into a vital and separate part of Masonic tradition for African-American

"TODAY'S MASONS MAINTAIN THEIR COMMITMENT TO ORAL TRADITION — THE PASSING OF KNOWLEDGE, EXPERIENCE, AND WISDOM FROM GENERATION TO GENERATION."

*Vintage portrait of a Shriner*

*Masonic silver medal*

men. Although African-American men today can join any lodge, Prince Hall has become a powerful incubator of Black leadership, as well as providing charitable support to the African-American community.

Experts attribute the fading interest in Freemasonry to a shift in modern-day leisure activities. The monthly meetings and associated time commitments carry less appeal to the techno-driven generations. In response, the lodges have begun to actively recruit younger men. The websites for individual lodges have become veritable marketing campaigns, offering candid answers to questions about what it means to be a Freemason, aiming to dispel any false rumors. The New York Lodge even hired a public relations firm to spread the word about its 225th anniversary in 2006. Other lodges have begun offering one-day classes to award the first three Masonic degrees in a single session, something that Masons years ago would have spent months earning.

Some Masons fear that standards have lowered in order to boost membership. However, the structured code that Masons live by is still grounded in the original tenets laid down by the stonemasons nearly three centuries ago. Today's Masons maintain their commitment to oral tradition—the passing of knowledge, experience, and wisdom from generation to generation. Members say it takes a brother to guide another brother in order to obtain the enlightenment that Masonry offers. Likewise, their quest to expand and do more good remains firm. The charitable works also continue through the 200 Masonic not-for-profit foundations, ranging from hospitals to charter

*Statue of George Washington, the quintessential Masonic hero*

schools, which donate millions each year.

Today the mainstream media largely focuses on the positive aspects of Masonry, and members speak candidly about the organization. The Freemasons offer tours of their lodges, opening their doors with the hope of inspiring younger generations to keep the traditions alive. The cherished artifacts, some of which are on display, preserve the Masons' long-standing tradition of remembering its past membership, heroes, and ancestry. The Grand Lodge in Boston protects the apron worn by General Lafayette

as well as the gavel George Washington used during a Masonic ceremony in 1793. Modern-day Masons regard Washington as the quintessential Masonic hero, distinguished by his indisputable integrity. Such artifacts serve as a bridge to the past, helping to perpetuate the history and the men that came before them.

Regardless of efforts to demystify the fraternity, the weight of negative publicity has continued to take its toll. The writings of former Mason, Frenchman Leo Taxis, during the 1880's still resonate today. According to Taxis,

Freemasons worshipped Lucifer, a dark secret known only to the most evolved of Freemasons. Even after confessing to his self-manufactured hoax in 1897, the myth wove itself into Masonic lore, later appearing in Pat Robertson's book *The New World Order*. These deeply embedded suspicions later fueled the controversy around William James' death in 2004 during a Masonic initiation ceremony. During James' induction, Albert Eid, a 77-year-old veteran, was to fire a pistol shot at some empty tin cans. Instead, he shot James. What was deemed a senseless

*Portrait of George Washington on U.S. currency*

*Above: Carving in Rosslyn Chapel. Freemasonry is believed to have begun among medieval stonemasons guilds, and now forms the cornerstone of many conspiracy theories.*

tragedy by the courts, only further dramatized the conspiracy theories. There is no doubt, say the skeptics, that the Freemasons control the justice system. It might be worth mentioning that Eid and James were the best of friends.

These stories serve to fuel the conspiracy theories. Various myths persist linking the Freemasons to the Holy Grail and identifying members as the descendants of the Knights Templar. In the 2004 film *National Treasure*, Nicolas Cage plays an archeologist in search of priceless artifacts that the Knights Templar passed on to the Freemasons, who then hid them during the American Revolution. It is a bona fide adventure, filled with conspiracies and secret codes, set against the backdrop of real history. If you ask a modern-day Mason to verify these speculations, you will most likely get a smile and chuckle. "It's not like we're sitting in here, polishing the Holy Grail every Thursday night when we meet," says David Johnson, a junior warden at the Scottish Rite Masonic Hall in Washington DC. "We drink out of the Holy Grail, but we don't polish it. It couldn't take it—it's very old."

The reality, it seems, is less mysterious than the veil of secrecy would lead you to believe. "Once you get through the romanticism of a quest that doesn't exist, or foolishness about the Knights Templar of the Arc of the Covenant or the Holy Grail, you find out that there really is a quest," says Mark Tabbert, author of *American Freemasons* and director of collections at the George Washington Masonic Lodge in Virginia, "and the quest is the inner journey, the self-improvement, is the desire to actually be useful in society and improve yourself."

It would seem that Freemasonry in the 21st century has become less of a "secret society," and more of a "society with secrets."

*A skull and crossbones*

# CHAPTER 6:

# SKULL & BONES

A STUDENT GROUP AT YALE UNIVERSITY,
SKULL AND BONES IS VIEWED AS THE
MOST INFLUENTIAL COLLEGIATE SOCIETY
IN THE UNITED STATES.

One night each year, 15 juniors at Yale University are "tapped" to join a 175 year old secret society. Senior members show up on doorsteps, pound loudly, and ask: "Skull and Bones, do you accept?" Those who do receive a message wrapped with a black ribbon sealed with black wax, displaying a crossbones and skull, its official emblem. Inside, instructions detail the time and location for the formal induction—at the Tomb.

The Tomb is a windowless brownstone building on the Yale campus, built in 1856. Home to the Skull and Bones members' meetings, it is reported to contain skulls, skeletons, coffins, and other macabre art and relics. The new initiates are rumored to undergo a two-part confessional experience. First they must share their life story, exposing their deepest traumas, fears and dreams, and then Part Two requires them to recount their sexual histories. These intimate disclosures have been known to disrupt romances across campus, as lovers are betrayed for the new allegiance that is Skull and Bones.

It may seem like just another college fraternity replete with silly antics, until you review the membership roster. Of all collegiate societies, Skull and Bones is regarded as the most influential in the nation. In 2004 the race for the United States' 41st Presidency featured two Bonesmen: Democratic Massachusetts Senator John Kerry and Republican George W. Bush. President Bush subsequently tapped five Bonesmen to join his administration, including William Donaldson as the head of the Securities and Exchange Commission. Influential indeed.

*Yale University campus in New Haven, Connecticut*

"'I THINK THERE IS A DEEP AND LEGITIMATE DISTRUST IN AMERICA FOR POWER AND PRIVILEGE THAT ARE CLOAKED IN SECRECY. IT'S NOT SUPPOSED TO BE THE WAY WE DO THINGS,' SAYS ACCLAIMED JOURNALIST RON ROSENBAUM."

*Demosthenes, the Greek orator, is thought to reside inside The Tomb*

The very roots of the society climb all the way to the top of the United States' power structure. In 1832, Alphonso Taft, father of future President William H. Taft, co-founded Skull and Bones with William Huntington Russell under the name of "The Order of Skull and Bones," later changed to "Skull and Bones." Russell had recently returned to Yale from Germany where he had been studying Hegelian philosophy, a worldview very much in vogue that deemed the individual obedient to the supreme state. Both fascism and communism have their roots in Hegel's doctrines. At the time Russell's family operated a firm called Russell

& Company, which not only served as the corporate name for Skull and Bones (listed as the Russell Trust Association) but also became the third largest opium dealer in the world. This notable historical link embeds the group's financial roots in one of the most scandalous ventures on record. Inspiring a long legacy of powerful men, Russell went on to become general of the U.S. Army and a state legislator, while Taft rose through the governmental ranks to the position of Secretary of War. The group from here continued to become a secret breeding ground for power, tucked in the very bosom of America's top collegiate institution.

Not surprisingly, then, this elite network has provoked endless suspicion among outsiders, inspiring many attempts to penetrate the Tomb's triple-padlocked iron door. Acclaimed journalist Ron Rosenbaum returned to his alma mater to explore his longtime fascination. A classmate of George W. Bush, Rosenbaum lived next door to the Tomb and recalls hearing "whispers and screams" emanating from within. "I think there is a deep and legitimate distrust in America for power and privilege that are cloaked in secrecy. It's not supposed to be the way we do things," says Rosenbaum. "We're supposed to do things out in the open in

*John Kerry (Bonesman '66)*

America. And so that any society or institution that hints that there is something hidden is, I think, a legitimate subject for investigation."

In 1876 a group calling itself "The Order of File and Claw" successfully broke into the Tomb, making their way to the inner sanctum: lodge room 322. This mystic numerical symbol appears on the Skull and Bones emblem, eliciting different interpretative meanings. Most conclude an allusion to the death of Greek orator Demosthenes in 322 BC. There inside, the intruders discovered a room bedecked in

red velvet with the German words written on it: *"Wer war der Thor, wer Weiser, wer Bettler oder Kaiser? Ob arm, ob reich, im Tode gleich,"* translated as, "Who was the fool, who the wise man, beggar or king? Whether poor or rich, all's the same in death."

This quotation provides a valuable insight into the society. A certain fixation on death permeates its secret ceremonies and rituals, requiring members to lie naked in coffins and kiss skulls. Supposedly, each class must also confiscate the bone relics of a famous individual

"SUPPOSEDLY, EACH CLASS MUST ALSO CONFISCATE THE BONE RELICS OF A FAMOUS INDIVIDUAL THAT ARE THEN DISPLAYED IN THE SKULL AND BONES MEETING HOUSE."

*George W. Bush (Bonesman '68)*

*Apache Indian Reservation; the tribal home of Chief Geronimo, whose bones were reportedly dug up and displayed in the Tomb*

☠ *A skull and crossbones carving on a cemetery wall*

that are then displayed in the Tomb. In 1918 Prescott Bush, the father of George H.W. Bush, allegedly robbed the grave of Apache chief Geronimo. As the story goes, Geronimo's grandson returned in 1989 to retrieve this stolen property. "There is still a glass case, Bonesmen tell me, within the Tomb that displays a skull that they all refer to as Geronimo," says Alexandra Robbins, a Yale graduate and author of *Secrets of the Tombs: Skull and Bones, the Ivy League, and the Hidden Paths of Power.*

Robbins persuaded approximately 100 Bonesmen to break their oaths of silence, thereby demystifying the rituals and secret ceremonies. According to her sources, the initiates are led into the room one at a time, and then once inside, the Bonesmen shriek at him. Finally, the Bonesman is shoved to his knees, at which point the senior Bonesman lifts his sword, taps the neophyte on his left shoulder and says, "By order of our order, I dub thee knight of Euloga." Once inducted, each member reportedly receives a $15,000 stipend and a grandfather clock, not to mention a bond that lasts for life. The vow of silence, forbidding any disclosure of the activities within, requires members to leave the room any time the name Skull and Bones is mentioned in public.

Conspiracy theories claim the society has agenda-based motives, pointing to the curious fact that members are initiated as juniors, thereby focusing on future-oriented activities. The Bonesmen meet twice a week, every Tuesday and Thursday, during their final academic year. "I believe the point of the year in the tomb is to forge such a strong bond

"UNION BANKING CORPORATION BECAME THE LEADING FINANCIAL INSTITUTION BETWEEN HITLER AND THE WORLD AT LARGE. THE BOARD MEMBERS INCLUDED TWO MEMBERS OF THE NAZI PARTY, AND THREE BONESMEN."

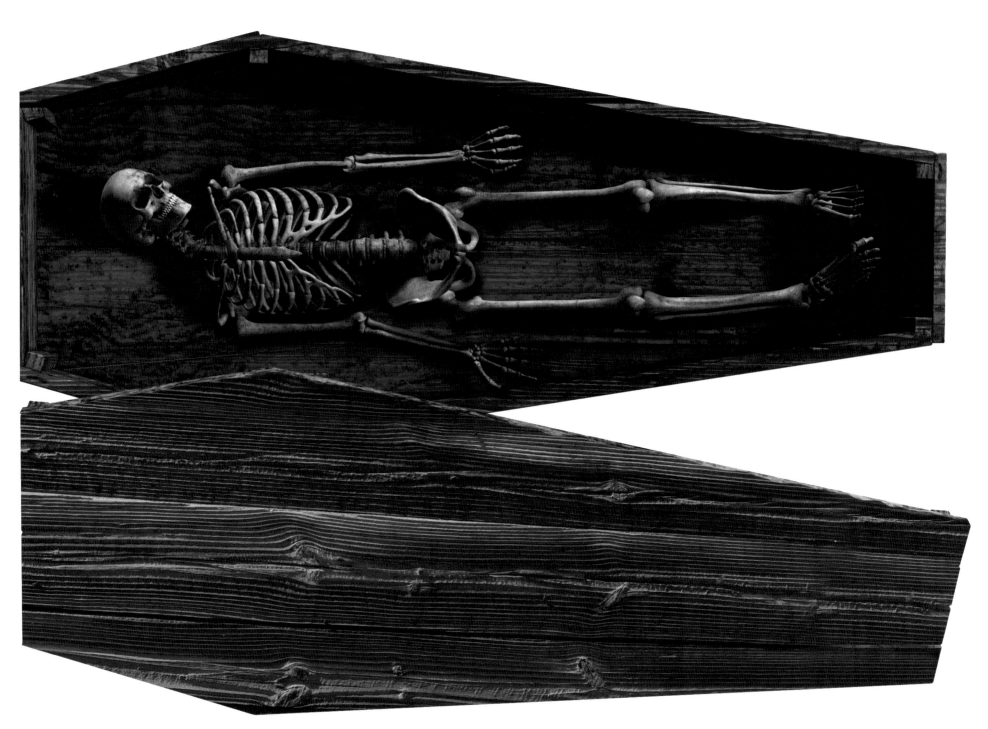

A fixation on death permeates the secret ceremonies and rituals, requiring members to lie naked in coffins and kiss skulls

between these 15 new members that after they graduate, for them to betray Skull and Bones would mean they'd have to betray 14 of their closest friends," says Robbins. The powers of influence stretch and expand well beyond graduation, linking Bonesmen to positions of authority, identified as key individuals who have helped shape world events. The most shocking and nefarious revelation has been the alleged association between Bonesmen and the financing behind the Nazi Party. According to John Lawrence Reynolds in his book *Secret Societies: Inside the World's Most Notorious Organizations*, by the mid-1930s the Union Banking Corporation (UBC) had become the leading financial institution between Hitler and the world at large. The UBC Board members not only included two members of the Nazi Party, but also Bonesmen E. Roland Harriman ('17), Knight Wooley ('17), Ellery S. James ('17) and Prescott S. Bush ('17).

The group has also served as fertile recruiting ground for the CIA, including author and secret agent William F. Buckley and former CIA director and 40th U.S. President George H.W. Bush. The recent Hollywood film *The Good Shepherd* has offered deeper insight into this link. The story follows Edward Wilson, an eager, optimistic student at Yale, who is tapped to join Skull and Bones, portrayed as a breeding ground for future world leaders. He is then soon recruited to work for ultra-secret Office of Strategic Services (OSS), the precursor to the CIA, during World War II. When the CIA was born, Wilson becomes an integral piece of its workings and development. Conspiracy buffs will be quick to tell you that three real-life CIA Bonesmen—Richard Drain ('43), William P. Bundy ('39) and McGeorge Bundy ('40)—masterminded the notorious Bay of Pigs incident in 1961. This event accelerated the rapid deterioration of Cuban-American

The Tomb is filled with skulls, bones and other macabre relics

# "IT IS WIDELY BELIEVED THAT THE SOLE PURPOSE OF SKULL AND BONES IS TO GET MEMBERS INTO POWER AND THEN TO HAVE THEM HIRE OTHER MEMBERS TO PROMINENT POSITIONS."

relations and paved the way to the Cuban Missile Crisis the following year.

While only 600–800 living members exist at any given time, this concentrated, tiny group has proven to be the ultimate boys' club—an unparalleled social and political network. It is widely believed that the sole purpose of Skull and Bones is to get members into positions of power and then to have those members hire other members to prominent positions. Henry Luce (the founder of Time Inc.), Supreme Court Justice Potter Stewart and J. Richardson Dilworth (manager of the Rockefeller fortune) are all former Bonesmen. Henry Stimson, Secretary of War under FDR, called his Skull and Bones experience the most profound of his entire education.

With such striking implications, one cannot help but wonder if it is mere coincidence, or if there exists within Skull and Bones an agenda to manipulate financial and political ends on a global scale.

As suspicions escalate, it is also impossible to overlook the significant positive contributions Bonesmen have made over the years. Many esteem its members' successes, giving the society credit for instilling a sense of public duty, moral leadership, and commitment within its ranks. "You take these young strivers, you put them in this weird castle. They spill their guts with each other, fine. But they learn something beyond themselves. They learn a commitment to each other, they learn a commitment to the community," says David Brooks, a columnist for The New York Times. "And maybe they inherit some of those old ideals of public service that are missing in a lot of other parts of the country."

In recent years the group has begun to embrace more diversity, tapping Jews and blacks by the early 50s, followed by homosexuals in the late 60s. However, it was not until 1992 that the society opened its doors to women, albeit with great resistance. "Skull and Bones narrowly endorsed admitting women," says Robbins. "The day before these women were supposed to be initiated, a group of Bonesmen, including William F. Buckley, obtained a court order to block the initiation, claiming that letting women into the tomb would lead to date rape." Now finally inside, women secured six of the 15 inductions in 2000.

Meanwhile, floating rumors suggest that juniors are more often declining invitations to join, indicating that the society is deflating in prestige. Regardless, Skull and Bones still maintains its reputation as the most secretive and exclusive of all Yale societies. Its activities, and their true nature, are still subject to debate— hidden behind a very thick skull.

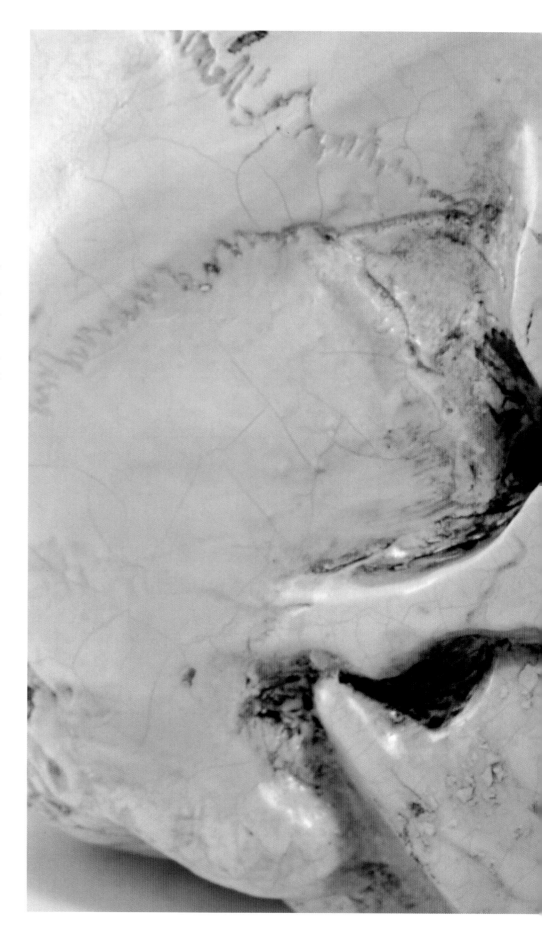

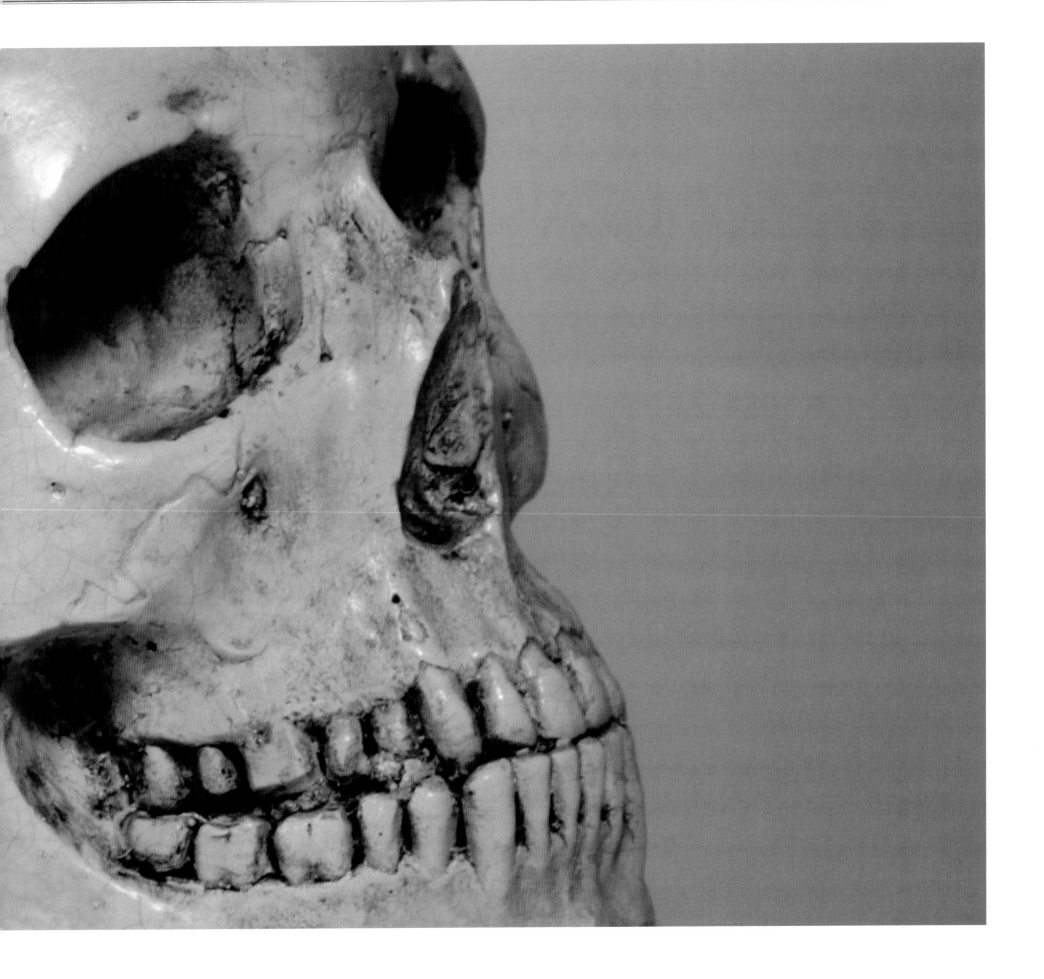

CHAPTER 7:

# KU KLUX KLAN

A noose

SELF-STYLED AS "THE INVISIBLE EMPIRE",
THE KLAN HAVE ATTACKED BLACKS, JEWS,
HOMOSEXUALS, CATHOLICS, IMMIGRANTS AND
ANYONE ELSE CONSIDERED FOREIGN.

In the dead of night, a small group of individuals dressed in white hoods and robes stand in a circular formation holding torches. Their leader, Grand Wizard Robert Miles, speaks: *"Welcome to the invisible empire, brothers and sisters. We hope that this sacred ritual will inspire a racial spirit in you as it does in us, and make you remember your heritage, your forefathers, that this symbol has been a part of throughout history."*

The word "symbol" refers to the cross, rooted at the center of the gathering. A man in black garb sets it aflame, as Miles asks his audience to lift their spirits and embrace the courage to recruit others to the movement. He calls for "an eventual victory that is ours"—a victory that calls for the achievement of white supremacy in the United States.

This scene, as shown in James Ridgeway's documentary *Blood in the Face*, offers a window into the secret society known as the Ku Klux Klan, one of the most notorious hate groups in America. They call themselves

"The Invisible Empire" and are distinguished by their strange disguises, silent parades, and midnight rides on horses also covered in white sheets. Originally targeted against Blacks, the Klan has also directed their violence towards Jews, homosexuals, Catholics, immigrants, and anyone else considered foreign. Their terrorizing tactics have included lynching, beatings, bombings, and murder.

It all began in 1866 in Pulaski, Tennessee. Six former Confederate soldiers gathered to discuss their opposition to the reconstruction policies after the Civil War. The Republican Congress had just established the Freeman's Bureau, which was designed to protect the interests of the newly emancipated slaves. This assistance included helping them find employment and improving their educational and health facilities.

In the year that followed, the bureau spent 17 million dollars establishing 4,000 schools and 100 hospitals, and providing homes and food for ex-slaves.

Carving of Confederate Generals at Stone Mountain, Georgia, USA

Lincoln Memorial: President Lincoln abolished slavery after the Civil War in 1865

The advancement of blacks posed a threat to these Southern men. In reaction they founded the Ku Klux Klan, a loosely organized, fraternal order bonding them in their common concern. Former Confederate General Nathan Bedford Forrest was appointed the first Grand Wizard, or overall leader of the Klan. They began mobilizing efforts to curb Black education, economic advancement, voting rights and the right to bear arms. Forrest then organized its spread to Alabama in 1868, a year when attacks on blacks became more common. When applying for membership, prospective candidates were asked to identify their political associations and to answer questions such as, "Are you opposed to Negro equality, both social and political?" and "Are you in favor of a white man's government?"

Soon, the Klan's secret power was undeniable, and any attempt to thwart it resulted in significant repercussions. In 1870 Governor William Holden of North Carolina endeavored to use state militia against the Klan, which led to his own impeachment from office. The Klan soon met with aggressive federal intervention, but the decentralized nature of the organization made membership difficult to prove. As a secret or "invisible" group, it had no membership rosters, no dues, no newspapers, no spokesmen, no chapters, no local officers, and no state or national officials. Congressional and legal investigations ensued, and a federal jury declared the Klan a terrorist organization. The Civil Rights Act of 1871 then followed, written by House Representative Benjamin Franklin Butler, which enforced the 15th Amendment protecting the citizens' right to vote. Under this Act, President Ulysses S. Grant took vigorous action against the Klan, forcing them to soon disband.

Neither racism nor the Klan disappeared in America—they were only temporarily suppressed. The 1890s maintained a

"Former Confederate General Nathan Bedford Forrest was appointed the first Grand Wizard, or overall leader of the Klan. They began mobilizing efforts to curb Black education, economic advancement, voting rights and the right to bear arms."

*Slave Market Building, Charleston*

romanticized vision of the Klan, as members reminisced about the days when they rode on horses to save the South from Negro domination. Lynchings were reportedly at a peak during this decade. The fear of being bred out of existence, of being the minority, continued to brew under the surface among the white southerners, building towards a resurgence much more potent and extensive.

The catalyst was Thomas Dixon's popular novel, *The Clansman*. Published in 1905, this work struck a chord in the latent yet burning prejudice. His words sent a message to Northerners to maintain racial segregation, claiming that Blacks turn savage when freed. Ten years later, D.W. Griffith's silent film *A Birth of a Nation* adapted the novel, portraying the Klan as a noble organization that had saved the Civil War-era South from the tyranny and corruption of southern Blacks and northern Republicans. The 1915 film created a nationwide craze for the terrorist organization, endorsed as well by President Woodrow Wilson. "The white men were roused by a mere instinct of self-preservation," wrote Wilson in his book *History of the American People*, "until at last there had sprung into existence a great KKK, a veritable empire of the South, to protect the Southern country."

To spur passions further, the case of Leo Frank hit the headlines. It involved a sexual crime against a woman named Mary Phagan. Frank was an American Jew whose sensational trial turned the spotlight on anti-Semitism. Georgian politician and publisher Tom E. Watson used the case to build support for the renewal of the KKK. When new evidence turned up calling Frank's guilt into question, a mob calling itself "the Knights of Mary

Leg irons

Phagan" kidnapped him from prison and hanged him. A month later, the Knights of Mary Phagan climbed Georgia's Stone Mountain and burned a giant cross, visible throughout the city of Atlanta. This image of the burning cross, a symbol of the original Klan, had been recently reintroduced by Griffith's film. A man by the name of William J. Simmons then returned to Stone Mountain with 34 men to light a second cross. This event signified the revival and official inauguration of the Klan, and Simmons thereby declared himself its Grand Wizard.

By now the Ku Klux Klan was more than a southern organization, it was a national phenomenon. In addition to white supremacy,

Simmons added anti-Semitism and anti-Catholicism to its agenda. He managed to attract the middle class in droves by promoting progressive reforms, including improved law enforcement, honest government, better public schools, and traditional family life. Unlike the original Klan, the second Klan was much more organized. Simmons acquired the original precepts written by George Gordon in 1868, which he used to write his own prospectus. As the Klan's public profile grew, so did its internal culture. Simmons created the hooded uniforms and an elaborate sacred ritual for the secret order. The mysterious language began to solidify bonds between Klansmen in the

form of acronyms. When greeting someone, a Klansman would say "AYAK," meaning, "Are you a Klansman?" A true Klansman would then reply, "AKIA," translated as, "A Klansman I am."

By the 1920s the Klan's membership peaked at 4–5 million. This number accounted for 15 percent of the nation's eligible voters. In 1922 Simmons handed the organization over to Hiram W. Evans, who turned it into a powerful political machine. It had become so influential that neither party would denounce it. The Klan managed to elect many state officials and Congressmen, wielding increasing control by infiltrating the government, primarily in

*Stone Mountiain, Atlanta*

*The lynching of Leo Frank*

*President Ulysses S. Grant took vigorous action against the Klan, forcing them to disband*

Tennessee, Oklahoma, and Oregon. Their seats of power included Bibb Graves as Governor of Alabama, Hugo Black to the U.S. Senate, and two Supreme Court Justices. Klan influence was particularly strong in Indiana, where Republican Edward Jackson was elected governor in 1924, successfully stocking the entire apparatus of state government with Klansmen.

During this period the government turned a blind eye to violence carried out by the Klan against Blacks, Catholics, Jews, and moral non-conformists. However, the press did not entirely back down in the face of the group's remarkable popularity and fierce powers of intimidation. Some journalists ventured to take a stand, Grover C. Hall for one. A journalist for Alabama's *Montgomery Advertiser*, Hall won the Pulitzer Prize for a series of editorials and articles he wrote attacking the Klan for racial and religious intolerance. Even so, the Klan remained largely immune to the criticism.

It was not until the downfall of David C. Stephenson that the Klan took a major hit, ending the "second wave" of Klan activity. Stephenson, the Grand Wizard of Indiana and 14 other states, was convicted of murder. The trial generated a sensational buzz. Charged with the rape and death of Madge Oberholtzer, this fallen Klan leader created a severe backlash against the Klan, whose membership suddenly dwindled to 30,000 by 1930. What followed was a decade of internal disputes, financial gaffes and legal probes. Evans eventually sold the Klan to James Colescott in 1939, and by 1944 the organization had disbanded due to depleted dues and financial resources.

Yet the terror and harrowing images had been forever imprinted in the minds of the American public, and would continue to wreak havoc for years to come. The statistics proved it. According to the Center for Constitutional Rights, between 1882 and 1968, mobs lynched

"David C. Stephenson, the Grand Wizard of Indiana and 14 other states, was convicted of murder. The trial generated a sensational buzz. Charged with the rape and death of Madge Oberholtzer, this fallen Klan leader created a severe backlash against the Klan"

*Montgomery, Alabama*

*The view from Georgia's Stone Mountain, home to the revival of the Ku Klux Klan in 1915*

4,743 persons in the United States, over 70 percent of them Black. Billie Holiday's signature song *"Strange Fruit"* would ultimately become the anthem for the anti-lynching movement. First recorded in 1939, the haunting lyrics and melody made it impossible for white Americans and politicians to continue to ignore the Southern campaign of racist terror.

The lyrics were originally a poem by Abel Meeropol, a Jewish schoolteacher and union activist from the Bronx, who later set them to music. It was first published in 1937 in *The New York Teacher*, a union magazine. Disturbed by Lawrence Beitler's 1930 photograph of the lynching of Thomas Shipp and Abram Smith, Meeropol wrote the stark verse under the

pseudonym Lewis Allan. Just two years later, Holiday's rendition struck a chord in American hearts, and is thought to have planted one of the first seeds of what would later become the Civil Rights Movement of the 1950s and 1960s.

The 1954 U.S. Supreme Court case, *Brown vs. Board of Education*, turned the heat on once again. This landmark decision called for desegregation, sparking a strong resistance to the federal legislation. It led to a massive rally in 1955 back atop Stone Mountain, with 3,500 in attendance. The Klan reemerged in the form of the White Knights led by Robert Shelton, and terror surged in full force, now blatantly assaulting Blacks and civil rights workers with beatings, bombings, death threats, and murder.

A burning cross, the Klan's trademark, was often stuck into the ground at the scene of Klan violence. The efforts to terrorize the Blacks into submission were remarkably effective. By 1960, Mississippi's population was 42 percent Black, with only 2 percent registered to vote.

The Klan stated its intentions "to protect" America from communism and the Civil Rights Movement, thereby justifying its numerous heinous crimes that now define this era of American history. "When you have to do the time," Grand Wizard Robert Miles told his fellow Klansmen, "don't regret the crime." On Sunday morning, September 15, 1963, the Klan bombed the Sixteenth Street Baptist Church in Birmingham, Alabama, killing four girls. Then

Map of Atlanta, Georgia

"IN 2005, 82-YEAR-OLD EDGAR RAY KILLEN, A FORMER KLAN LEADER, WAS CONVICTED FOR THE DEATHS OF THREE CIVIL RIGHTS WORKERS IN MISSISSIPPI. HE WAS SENTENCED TO THREE CONSECUTIVE 20-YEAR PRISON TERMS."

on June 21, 1964, three young civil rights workers—James Chaney, Andrew Goodman, and Michael Schwerner—were murdered in Nashoba County, Mississippi. They had been working to register Black voters in Mississippi during Freedom Summer and had gone to investigate the burning of a Black church. They were arrested by the police on trumped-up charges, imprisoned for several hours, and then released after dark into the hands of the Ku Klux Klan, who beat and murdered them. It was later proven in court that a conspiracy existed between the local law enforcement and the Klan to kill them.

These murderous acts shocked the nation and further galvanized the Civil Rights Movement. The FBI started to infiltrate the Klan, and by the 1970s, managed to crack down on their operations. Soon the Klan's membership dwindled to a few thousand. The steady decline

has continued to the present day, due to failure to recruit younger extremists, hefty litigation expenses, and strong law enforcement. Recent years have brought justice to some historic crimes. In 2000 the Cahaba Boys, a splinter group of the Klan, were convicted of the Sixteenth Street Baptist Church bombing, resulting in the sentence of Bobby Cherry to life in prison. Then in 2005, 82-year-old Edgar Ray Killen, a former Klan leader, was convicted for the deaths of the three civil rights workers in Mississippi. He was sentenced to three consecutive 20-year prison terms.

Still, the criminal acts persist, requiring law enforcement to stay on its toes. In 1981 Josephus Andersonan, an African-American man, was charged with the murder of a white policeman in Mobile, Alabama. At the end of the trial, the jury was unable to reach a verdict, upsetting members of the Ku Klux Klan who pointed to the Black jury members as the reason. At a post-trial meeting, Bennie Hays, the second-highest ranking official in the Klan in Alabama said: "If a black man can get away with killing a white man, we ought to be able to get away with killing a black man." Shortly thereafter Bennie Hays's son, Henry Hays, and James Knowles kidnapped Michael Donald, a 19-year-old African-American man. After forcing him into the car, they took Donald to the next county and lynched him. The Southern Poverty Law Center used this case to destroy the Klan in Alabama. The civil suit against the United Klans of America took place in February 1987. The all-white jury found the Klan responsible for the lynching of Michael Donald and ordered it to pay 7 million dollars, closing their operations down. After a long-drawn-out legal struggle, Henry Hays was finally executed in 1997. It was the first time a white man had been executed for a crime against a Black person since 1913.

Ku Klux Klan members in their hooded uniforms

*The burning cross is a trademark of the KKK, often stuck in the ground at the site of Klan violence*

To this day, watchdog efforts extend across state lines and inside the federal government. In 2003 the Supreme Court upheld a Virginia law that makes cross burning an act of intimidation. At the same time, the American Civil Liberties Union (ACLU) has provided legal support in defense of the Klan's peaceful activism, defending the First Amendment right to hold public rallies, parades, and marches, as well as their right to field political candidates.

Many believe the Ku Klux Klan is unlikely ever to disappear. Hot-button issues such as immigration, gay marriage, and urban crime, when successfully exploited, generate considerable public support for Klan ideology. The popularity of former Klansman David Duke is a prime example. In the 1990s Duke brought overt racism to mainstream politics in the South, styling himself as a "racial realist." In favor of racial segregation and white separatism, he believes that all people have a basic human right to preserve their own heritage. Duke ran for President of the United States in 1988 on the Populist Party ticket, and won 23,000 votes in Louisiana. The next year he was elected to the Louisiana state legislature.

Early on, Duke successfully marketed himself as a new brand of Klansman, well groomed and professional. In 1974, he founded the Louisiana-based Knights of the Ku Klux Klan, shortly after graduating from Louisiana State University. He attempted to reform the organization by promoting nonvisiblee and legality. He wanted to modernize the Klan and turn it into a legitimate political force. For example, he changed the title of "Grand

An Amercian Nazi Party rally in Seattle; like the Ku Klux Klan, it calls for white supremacy

*The fight against racism continues*

Wizard" to "National Director" and sported a business suit instead of a white robe—the same man, by the way, who was famous in college for wearing a Nazi uniform while picketing and holding parties on Adolf Hitler's birthday. The Klan enjoyed a rebirth under Duke's leadership. In 1976, he organized a rally in Walker, Louisiana, the largest the nation had witnessed since the 1960s with an estimated 2,700 in attendance. He also built up local organizations in other states, including California, Florida, and Texas. He declared his intentions in the November 1978 issue of the *Crusader*, the KKK newspaper: "Our clear goal must be the advancement of the white race and separation of the white and black races. This goal must include freeing of the American media and government from subservient Jewish interests."

Duke abruptly left the Klan in 1978 when a rival reportedly caught him on videotape selling the Klan's highly secret membership list for US $35,000. Two years later he went on to found the National Association for the Advancement of White People (NAAWP), gradually moving himself and his agenda into mainstream politics, making him the highest profile white supremacist in the last two decades. In a letter to his followers, he wrote that NAAWP "avoids the Hollywood stereotypes and misconceptions about the Klan" and maintained that the messages of the two groups were "essentially the same." It is widely believed that Duke has merely camouflaged his racist ideas in a language and an image acceptable to the public. He, in effect, pioneered what has become a common tactic of the far right to appeal to race and class resentments.

The Ku Klux Klan maintains its Invisible Empire today through its far-reaching tentacles in people like David Duke, and various splinter and extremist groups. Although the Klan's current membership is only an estimated 2,500-3,000, a 2006 statement issued by the Anti-Defamation League reports the Klan to be alive and well: "Klan groups have witnessed a surprising and troubling resurgence by exploiting fears of an immigration explosion, and the debate over immigration has in turned helped to fuel an increase in Klan activity, with new groups sprouting in parts of the country that have not seen much activity."

Is it possible that this secret society is on the rebound? Best to keep an eye on Stone Mountain.

*The Klan marching through Washington in 1928*

*Trail through the Redwood Forest*

# CHAPTER 8:

# BOHEMIAN GROVE

>→·⊢◆→·○·←◆·⊣←

THE CLUB WAS FOUNDED IN 1872 TO "PROMOTE
SOCIAL AND INTELLECTUAL INTERCOURSE"
BETWEEN ITS MEMBERS—WHO NOW INCLUDE
MANY OF THE WORLD'S MOST INFLUENTIAL MEN

>→·⊢◆→·○·←◆·⊣←

Harry Shearer's Hollywood film *Teddy Bears' Picnic* takes place at Zambesi Glen, a fictional private compound where the richest and most powerful men gather for a rollicking good time. The tagline reads: "For 51 weeks a year they run the free world. For one week they run amok." This tongue-in-cheek comedy in fact closely resembles the real life men's club called Bohemian Grove—a virtual *Who's Who* of the most influential men in business and government.

Each year the world's elite descends upon California for a summer retreat at Bohemian Grove, 80 miles north of San Francisco. There they spend two weeks encamped on 2,700 acres of the pristine and privately owned Redwood forest, underneath its lush canopy.

The cliffs with 300–400-foot drops extend from the banks of Sonoma County's Russian River. This ultra-exclusive group of members and their guests enjoy a time of fun and games, harking back to the days of childhood summer camp. It is a rich man's playground, replete with gourmet camp grub, mock pagan pageantry and the highest level of networking on the planet. Herbert Hoover called it "the world's greatest men's party."

And quite an impressive party it is. The approximately 2,000 members have included every United States Republican President since 1923. Drawn in large part as well from the corporate leadership of America, the roster includes CEOs and directors from major corporations in every sector of the economy

Bohemian Grove extends from the banks of California's Russian River

"WHILE THE LOCATION IS WIDELY KNOWN,
THE ACTIVITIES ARE SHROUDED IN SECRECY."

whether it be oil, military, utilities, or banking. In an intensive 1991 study, sociologist Peter Philips listed corporations with more than three directors in attendance, citing Bank of America (7), Pacific Gas & Electric (5), AT&T (4), General Motors (3) and Ford Motor Company (3). German Chancellor Helmut Schmidt, an invited guest, referred to it as "the West's hidden summit."

The "invitation only" requirement judges prospective members by occupation, social standing and personal connections. The guest list, however, is highly secret and reputed to be a fascinating document. It reveals the network and personal connections between attendees, thereby providing a detailed map of the cliques and friendship patterns of the country's ruling circles. The bylaws of the Bohemian Club also stipulate that at least 100 members of the club be "connected professionally" with literature, art, music, or drama.

This affiliation with the arts dates back to the group's roots. The society was founded in 1872 by a group of San Francisco artists, who wanted a place to go to enjoy their talents. The founding statement outlined the group's profile and intentions to be "the promotion of social and intellectual intercourse between journalists and other writers, artists, actors and musicals, professional or amateur, and such others not included in this list as may by reason of knowledge and appreciation of polite literature and the fine arts be worthy of membership." The founding members included Ambrose Bierce, author of the humorous semi-classic *The Devil's Dictionary*, and poet Charles Warren Stoddard. Other notable writers soon

joined the group, such as Bret Harte, Mark Twain, and Jack London.

From the get-go, the Bohemian Club also embraced men with "money as well as brains." These artists knew it would take resources to realize their ambitions. As one of the original members wrote in his memoirs: "It was apparent that the possession of talent, without money, would not support the club." In little time, the Bohemian Club attracted the richest men in San Francisco and was listed in all the social registers of the era. When land developers were scouting the Redwood acreage, the Bohos, as they like to call themselves, decided to buy the land. They originally bought 160 acres, which by 1944 increased to the 2,700 acres of land that they own today. Yet the same material resources that nurtured the group also rattled its authenticity. By 1890, the early members began to express dismay that the club had lost its original salty spirit, washed out by commercialism. As Oscar Wilde put it: "I have never seen so many well-dressed, well-fed, business-like looking bohemians in my life." In 1905, a visit by Teddy Roosevelt was reported in the press, catapulting Bohemia forward to the highly elite group that it has now become over a century later.

The club hosts year-round activities but is most famous for its annual retreat in July. While the location is widely known, the activities are shrouded in secrecy, patrolled by helicopters and other security around the Grove's perimeter. Privacy is a virtue. Attendees are not permitted to write about, speak about, or videotape any activities, and the press is an unwelcome guest. However, many leaders in the media industry

"THE OPENING CEREMONY, CALLED 'THE CREMATION OF CARE,' IS MADE UP OF MEN DRESSED IN POINTED RED HOODS AND RED FLOWING ROBES, CARRYING AN OPEN COFFIN, INSIDE OF WHICH IS A FIGURE THAT LOOKS LIKE A HUMAN BODY."

participate and have been known to include William Randolph Hearst Jr., Jack Howard and Charles Scripps (Scripps-Howard) and Tom Johnson (former President of CNN and publisher of the *Los Angeles Times*).

Upon arrival, the men get settled into their appropriate camps, comprised of large log cabin-style homes built into the gorge walls. Over the years the sites have evolved from simple pitched tents to semi-luxury accommodations. Today there are about 120 camps of varying sizes, structures and status, sporting names like "Cliff Dwellers," "Moonshiners" and "Silverado Squatters." Most have between 10 and 30 members, but a few boast as many as 125. "Mandalay" is by far the most prestigious, whose all-star

cast includes George Shultz, Henry Kissinger, businessman Leonard Firestone, Gerald Ford, and William French Smith. "Cave Man" also carries a distinguished roster, boasting former Presidents Herbert Hoover and Richard Nixon. Ronald Reagan belonged to "Owl's Nest," while the Bush family resides in the "Hillbillies" alongside Walter Cronkite, William F. Buckley and A.W. Clausen of the World Bank. It has been described as a "overgrown Boy-scout camp" equipped with tram buses for those who enjoy convenience—a kind of rusticity mixed with luxury, not to mention extreme privilege.

The opening ceremony, called "The Cremation of Care," is made up of men dressed in pointed red hoods and red flowing robes, carrying an open coffin, inside of which is a figure that looks like a human body. Funeral music plays while a spectacular display of flames resonates against the forest backdrop. It is no surprise that this scene has provoked conspiracy alarmists, who make accusations of satanic worship and child sacrifice. Experts such as sociologist G. William Domhoff, author of bestseller *Who Rules America*, discredit these indictments as highly misconstrued, explaining that the mock ritual is more of a spoof. According to Dumhoff, secret huts, especially men's huts, go back to the beginnings of human history and to preadolescence as well. The Grove's strange ceremony has marked every gathering since 1880, asking the men to forget worldly cares. Its intention is to ease everyone into the mood so they can relax and enjoy themselves.

As the ceremony unfolds, Mr. Dull Care is ultimately cremated before a large altar featuring a 40-foot owl statue. The owl is the totem animal of the Bohemian Club, regarded as wise and discreet, and accessorizes everything from owl pins, ice buckets, ties, and denim shirts. During the club's mock Druidic rituals, the high priest falls to his knees and lifts his

*Accomodation at the Bohemian Grove is in a number of named camps*

A mural commemorating Jack London, an early member of the Bohemian Club

*St. John of Nepomuk, the patron saint of Bohemia*

arms to the shrine and mighty owl, asking, "Oh thou, great symbol of all mortal wisdom. Owl of Bohemia, we do beseech thee, grant us thy counsel." At this point, an aura of light appears around the owl's head, and the owl responds with, "Hail, Fellowship. Begone, Dull Care! Midsummer sets us free!" If you were attending Bohemian Grove in the 1990s, you would have recognized the owl's voice as none other than Walter Cronkite, a longtime member of the club. Ultimately, it is the owl that has the power to banish "Dull Care" ending the ceremony in a

climax of intensifying flames, orchestral music and a great fanfare of fireworks and explosions. "It's straight out of tribal life the world over," says Dumhoff. "No women. Lots of drinking and boasting. Men will be men, and boys will be boys."

Over the two-week encampment, the guests are treated to plays, variety shows, song fests, shooting contests, art exhibits, boating and nature rides. Of all these activities, the most elaborate are the two stage productions, referred to as the "High Jinks" and the "Low Jinks."

Both are elaborate productions with large stage sets, huge casts (75-100 people) and a budget of US $130,000-$150,000 according to the 2004 reports. These grandiose spectacles are written and produced by club members, and despite the extraordinary manpower and cost, each play is a unique one-time production that requires a yearlong preparation. The High Jinks tends to be a mannered and ponderous play, tackling mythical or fantasy themes, such as the legend of St. John of Nepomuk, the Patron Saint of Bohemia. Canonized for honor, St. John lived

The owl is the totem animal of Bohemian Grove

"THE GROVE'S MOTTO ASKS MEMBERS TO REFRAIN FROM DISCUSSING BUSINESS MATTERS. THAT SAID, MOST EVERYONE AGREES THAT THE MOST IMPORTANT BUSINESS THAT TAKES PLACE AT THE GROVE IS POLITICAL. "

in the real Bohemia of the 13th century, now part of the present-day Czech Republic. Other titles include *"The Fall of Pompeii," "Rip Van Winkle"* and *"The Rout of the Philistines."* It is considered the most formal event of the retreat. By contrast, the Low Jinks is an original musical comedy, known to be markedly lowbrow. Since no women are permitted in the Bohemian Club, men dress in drag and play women's parts. In 1989, the men playing women were nicknamed "heifers," inspiring the audience to moo each time the heifers entered onstage. Now that's entertainment.

The Grove's motto is, *"Weaving Spiders Come Not Here!"* This line from Shakespeare's *A Midsummer Night's Dream* asks members to refrain from discussing business matters, and instead to focus on literature and other pleasures within the oasis that is Bohemia. That said, most everyone agrees that the most important business that takes place at the Grove is political.

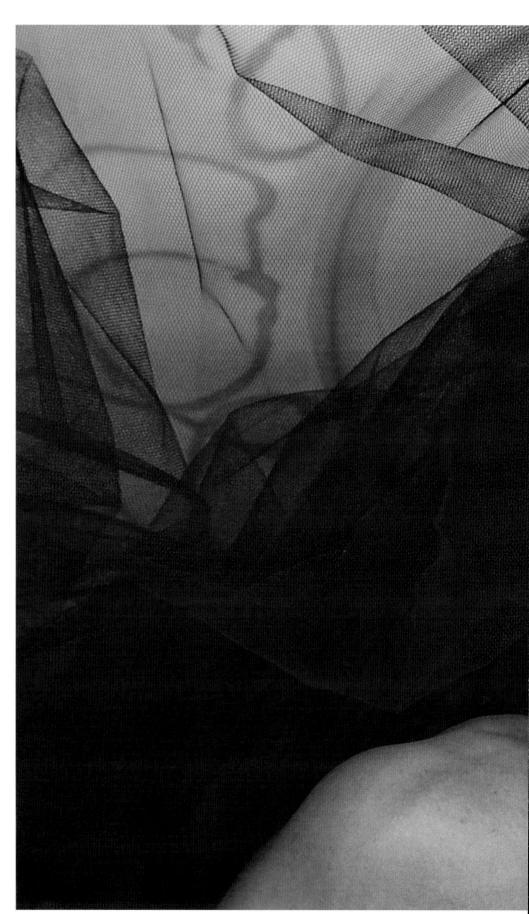

Since no women are allowed, men dress in drag for the stage productions

*California Redwoods*

"IN THE 1970S THE BOHEMIAN GROVE ACTION NETWORK (BGAN) WAS FORMED TO CHALLENGE THE ELITISM AND SECRECY, CLAIMING THAT POLICY DECISIONS ARE BEING MADE WITHOUT PUBLIC SCRUTINY."

Every afternoon the members enjoy intellectual stimulation and political enlightenment in the form of Lakeside Talks. It has been a way for politicians to float policy ideas without public scrutiny, and according to Richard Nixon, also a great opportunity to get a campaign rolling. "If I were to choose the speech that gave me the most pleasure and satisfaction in my political career, it would be my Lakeside Speech at the Bohemian Grove in July 1967," Nixon wrote in his memoirs published in 1978. "Because this speech traditionally was off the record it received no publicity at the time. But in many important ways it marked the first milestone on my road to the presidency." Nixon reportedly convinced Reagan to stay out of the Republican primaries that year, clearing his path for election. Today sitting Presidents are banned from attending. After his two-term in office, Reagan returned to the Grove saying, "It's good to be back."

At the 1991 retreat, the Grove enjoyed quite an impressive line-up of Lakeside speakers, including the African-American lawyer Vernon Jordan, former German Chancellor Helmut Schmidt and Attorney General Elliott Richardson. The then-Secretary of Defense Richard Cheney gave a speech titled "Major Defense Problems of the 21st Century," and George Shultz, the Secretary of State under Reagan, shared his "Agenda for America." It is known to be a forum where high-ranking officials divulge information that wouldn't otherwise be communicated to the public. Here is where some outsiders draw the line.

In the 1970s the Bohemian Grove Action Network (BGAN) was formed to challenge the elitism and secrecy, claiming that policy decisions are being made without public scrutiny. Founded by activist Mary Moore, BGAN has attracted over 70 left-wing activist groups into its fold. Each year the protestors congregate in Monte Rio, just outside of Bohemian Grove, during the two-week retreat. It includes leaders from the peace, environmental and immigrant rights movements. The protests reached a peak in 2001 with 1,000 people.

The club's anti-women policy has also generated legal recriminations. Charged with sex discrimination, the club employs a few women in its San Francisco headquarters, but bars them from working at the actual summer retreat. This policy infringes upon California's Civil Rights Act as well as San Francisco's Civil Rights Ordinance, and cannot be justified by privacy rights of the club members. When so many members participate for business-related reasons, it is difficult to prove that they are purely a private club that falls outside of the legal definition of a business. However, as reported by the *New York Times* in 1981, Judge Robert Kendall did underline that "the presence of women would alter the behavior of the members," citing the tendency of members to urinate in the open. After all, it is a long-standing Bohemian tradition.

For the time being, the admittance of women appears unlikely. And for those men who aspire to become members, be forewarned, the waiting list is a long one. Apparently, hundreds of prospective Bohemians are backed up to become regular resident members, patiently awaiting that letter of acceptance in the mail.

It reads: "You have joined not only a club, but a way of life."

129

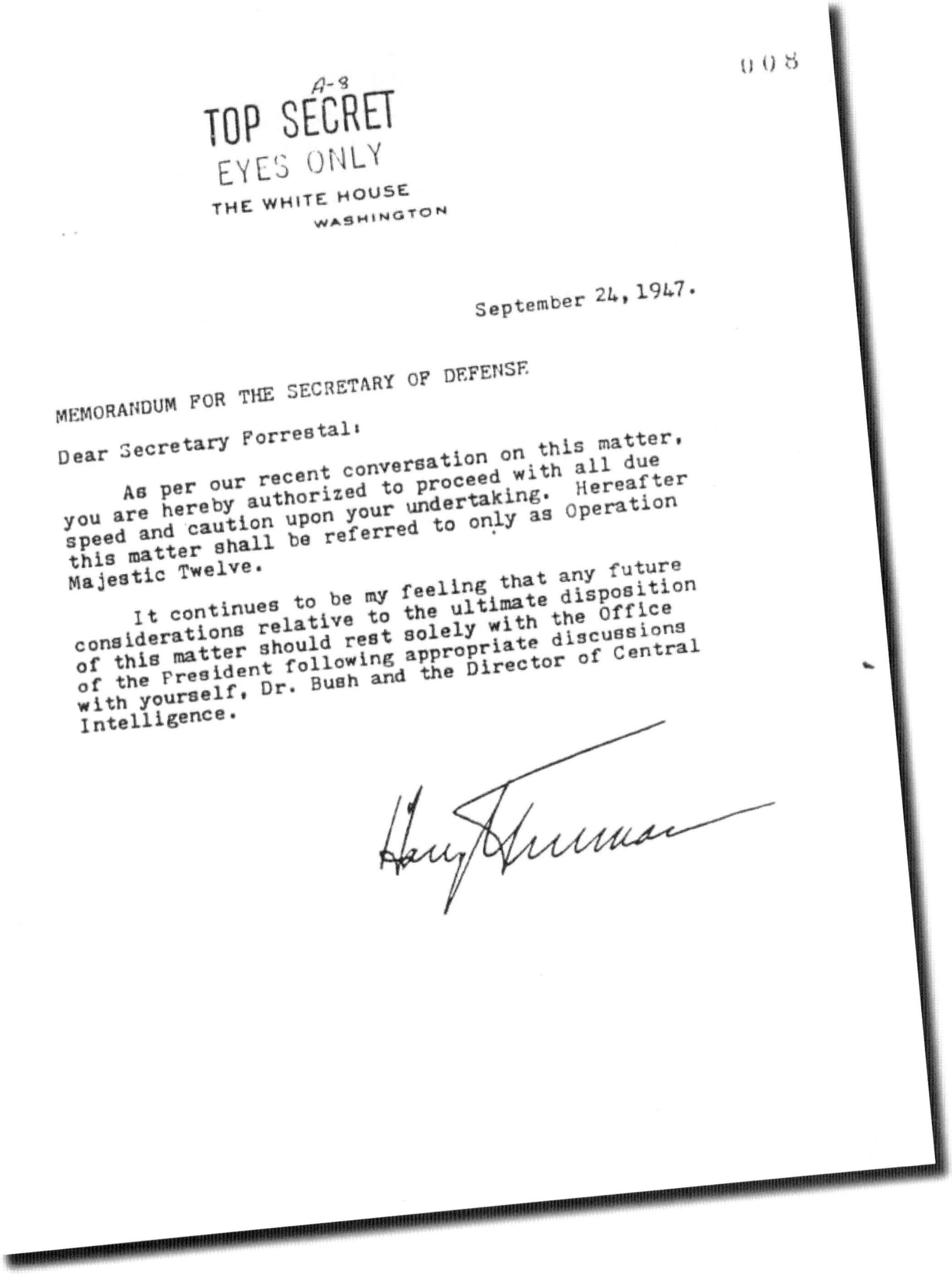

008

TOP SECRET

*A-3*

EYES ONLY

THE WHITE HOUSE

WASHINGTON

September 24, 1947.

MEMORANDUM FOR THE SECRETARY OF DEFENSE

Dear Secretary Forrestal:

As per our recent conversation on this matter, you are hereby authorized to proceed with all due speed and caution upon your undertaking. Hereafter this matter shall be referred to only as Operation Majestic Twelve.

It continues to be my feeling that any future considerations relative to the ultimate disposition of this matter should rest solely with the Office of the President following appropriate discussions with yourself, Dr. Bush and the Director of Central Intelligence.

*Harry Truman*

*The 1947 letter, allegedly signed by President Harry Truman, authorizing Operation Majestic 12*

# CHAPTER 9:

# MAJESTIC 12

ALSO KNOWN AS MJ 12, THE VERY EXISTENCE
OF THIS SECRET GROUP IS SUBJECT TO HEATED
DEBATE AMONG CONSPIRACY BUFFS.

On July 8, 1947, *The Roswell Daily Record* printed an astonishing headline: "RAAF Captures Flying Saucer on Ranch in Roswell Region." The newspaper was responding to a press release issued by the Roswell Army Air Field in New Mexico. It was based on debris that Major Jesse Marcel, an intelligence officer for the 509th Bomber Group, had discovered and collected as evidence. The story quickly spread, igniting a UFO craze that swept the country.

The excitement, however, soon subsided. General Roger Ramey held a press conference, explaining that the recovered debris was actually the remains of a weather balloon. For the next 40 years, the Roswell incident was largely a dead subject.

Then, in 1987, UFOlogist William L. Moore and two associates made public three "top secret" documents that revealed an alleged

government UFO conspiracy. The documents claimed that President Harry Truman had created a supersecret group called "Majestic 12" to handle the official cover-up of the Roswell crash in 1947. The primary record is a memo from President Harry Truman to Defense Secretary James Forrestal, dated September 24, 1947, which authorized its formation. Also known as MJ 12, this group is reportedly a secret committee of scientists, military leaders, and government officials whose purpose was to investigate UFO activity in the aftermath of the crash.

As the story goes, the documents were delivered in December 1984 to Jamie Shandera, a documentary filmmaker, in the form of two rolls of undeveloped film. From what Shandera concluded, an anonymous source had leaked the classified information. He subsequently enlisted the help of William Moore and Stanton

By financing its operations through illegal drug trafficking, MJ 12 remains out of the public eye and hidden from U.S. Congressmen.

Friedman, two prominent UFO researchers, who made the files public at the 24th Annual UFO Conference in Burbank, California.

The second document is a briefing report for President-elect Dwight D. Eisenhower, prepared by Admiral R.H. Hillenkoetter, who had been a director of the CIA and purportedly now the head of MJ 12. Dated November 18, 1952, it detailed the recovery, analysis, and official cover-up of the Roswell crash. The memo listed the names of the MJ 12 members. It consisted of 12 men selected from a larger umbrella organization called the Jason Society, which comprised the 32 most prominent Americans. Reportedly, MJ 12 is the secret control group within the Jason Society and is structured to operate outside of the American democratic system. It is believed that operations are financed through illegal drug trafficking. In this way, MJ 12 remains out of the public eye and hidden from U.S. Congressmen. According to the Eisenhower brief, the MJ 12 members included:

**Lloyd V. Bernkener:**
a physicist and engineer; member of the President's Scientific Advisory Committee; executive secretary of Vannevar Bush's JRDB.

**Dr. Detlev W. Bronk:**
a medical physicist and aviation physiologist; Chairman, National Academy of Sciences, National Research Council.

**Vannevar Bush:**
an engineer and scientist known for his political role in developing the atomic bomb; created the Joint Research and Development Board (JRDB), which promoted scientific research through the military.

**James V. Forrestal:**
Secretary of Defense; Walter Bedell Smith, 2nd CIA director, assumed his position in MJ 12 upon his death.

**Gordon Gray:**
Secretary of the Army; intelligence and national security expert.

**Rear Adm. Roscoe H. Hillenkoetter:**
first CIA director.

**Hoyt S. Vanderberg:**
Air Force Chief of Staff; succeeded Souers as Director of the Central Intelligence Group.

**Dr. Jerome C. Hunsaker:**
an aeronautical scientist and engineer; Chairman of the National Advisory Committee for Aeronautics.

**Dr. Donald H. Menzel:**
Harvard-educated astronomer and astrophysicist; security consultant to the CIA and the National Security Agency (NSA).

**Maj. Gen. Robert M. Montague:**
Guided missiles expert; Commander at Sandia Base, New Mexico.

**Rear Adm. Sidney W. Souers:**
First Director of the Central Intelligence Group; first executive secretary of National Security Council (NSC).

**Gen. Nathan F. Twining:**
Head of the Air Materiel Command at Wright-Patterson Air Force Base.

In the late 1940s, all of these men were at the top of their respective areas of expertise, each with high-level government experience. Furthermore, many had been navigating the

*Alleged UFO sighted in New Jersey in 1952*

TOP SECRET / MAJIC
*A-2*

EYES ONLY
* TOP SECRET *
••••••••••••••

COPY ONE OF ONE.

EYES ONLY

SUBJECT: OPERATION MAJESTIC-12 PRELIMINARY BRIEFING FOR
    PRESIDENT-ELECT EISENHOWER.

DOCUMENT PREPARED 18 NOVEMBER, 1952.

BRIEFING OFFICER: ADM. ROSCOE H. HILLENKOETTER (MJ-1)

NOTE: This document has been prepared as a preliminary briefing
only. It should be regarded as introductory to a full operations
briefing intended to follow.

• • • • • •

OPERATION MAJESTIC-12 is a TOP SECRET Research and Development/
Intelligence operation responsible directly and only to the
President of the United States. Operations of the project are
carried out under control of the Majestic-12 (Majic-12) Group
which was established by special classified executive order of
President Truman on 24 September, 1947, upon recommendation by
Dr. Vannevar Bush and Secretary James Forrestal. (See Attachment
"A".) Members of the Majestic-12 Group were designated as follows:

Adm. Roscoe H. Hillenkoetter
Dr. Vannevar Bush
Secy. James V. Forrestal*
Gen. Nathan F. Twining
Gen. Hoyt S. Vandenberg
Dr. Detlev Bronk
Dr. Jerome Hunsaker
Mr. Sidney W. Souers
Mr. Gordon Gray
Dr. Donald Menzel
Gen. Robert M. Montague
Dr. Lloyd V. Berkner

The death of Secretary Forrestal on 22 May, 1949, created
a vacancy which remained unfilled until 01 August, 1950, upon
which date Gen. Walter B. Smith was designated as permanent
replacement.

••••••••••••••
* TOP SECRET *
••••••••••••••

TOP SECRET / MAJIC

EYES ONLY

EYES ONLY

T52-EXEMPT (E)

002

68)

*The authenticity of the "Majestic-12" documentation has been hotly debated*

*Harry S. Truman, the 33rd President of the United States (1945-1953)*

UFO field of study. Both Vandenberg and Twining supervised early U.S. Air Force extraterrestrial investigations, such as Project Blue Book, and had made public statements on the subject. Twining had allegedly written a famous memo urging the government to launch a formal investigation of flying saucers. It was dated the day before Truman created MJ 12. Ten years later, Hillenkoetter joined the board of NICAP (National Investigations Committee On Aerial Phenomena), a powerful UFO civilian organization.

One name stood out, however, as a great shock. Donald Menzel had earned a reputation as a prominent skeptic of UFOs. As a well-respected scientist, his opinion had a great influence on mainstream opinion. He authored three popular books debunking UFOs: *Flying Saucers* (1953), *The World Of Flying Saucers:*

*A Scientific Examination of a Major Myth of the Space Age* (1963), and *The UFO Enigma: The Definitive Explanation of the UFO Phenomenon* (1977). In all cases, Menzel argued that UFO sightings were nothing more than misidentifying natural phenomena. His arguments pointed to atmospheric hazes and temperature inversions that might distort the perception of the stars or planets. In 1968, Menzel even testified before the U.S. House Committee on Science and Astronautics—Symposium on UFOs, stating that he considered all UFO sightings to have natural explanations. Why would Menzel then be listed as a member of MJ 12? His harshest critics denounced his debunking theories as laughable. Friedman later concluded that Menzel's writing must have been a deliberate attempt to reduce public and professional interest in UFOs.

As for the third document, Moore and Shandera had discovered it during a visit to the National Archives. Dated July 14, 1954, it is a short memo from Robert Cutler to General Twining, Chief of Staff of the U.S. Armed Forces, informing him that an MJ 12 meeting had been rescheduled. The subject heading was listed as "NSC/MJ 12 Special Studies Project." The National Archives subsequently received numerous inquiries about the memo's authenticity. A statement was then issued verifying that such a document exists, but that the National Archives could not certify its legitimacy.

The authenticity of all three documents has been hotly debated over the years. Not one of the MJ 12 members is alive today to question. In fact, the most recent death, that of Jerome Hunsaker, occurred just three months before

*Aerial shot of Area 51*

THE RECORDS DETAILED HOW MILITARY
CREWS SHOULD RECOVER CRASHED
SAUCERS AND THEIR EXTRATERRESTRIAL
CREWS, AND INSTRUCTED ALL REMAINS
TO BE SHIPPED TO "AREA 51."

Shandera claimed to receive the records. It was clear that someone waited until no alleged members could make any statements about their involvement.

A long-time investigator of UFO incidents, Philip Klass, has written several books separating the facts from the myths, including *The Real Roswell Crashed Saucer Cover-up*. His detailed research aggressively debunks each one of the Majestic 12 documents. He claims that Truman's signature is actually a pasted-on photocopy of a genuine signature lifted from a different memo. In the Eisenhower briefing, he notes the unusual formatting that curiously resembles the formatting William Moore used in his personal correspondence. It also makes reference to what Klass identifies as the "bogus" Truman document. Furthermore, on the date that Cutler allegedly wrote the memo to Twining, Cutler was in fact out of the country—not to mention that the document was found in an unlikely location at the National Archives.

The three documents were forwarded to British UFOlogist Timothy Good, who reproduced them in his best-selling book *Above Top Secret*. The files thus became widely known,

but Good later denounced them as fraudulent. At the urging of Klass, the FBI launched its own investigation. The AFOSI (U.S. Air Force Office of Special Investigations) was contacted to verify whether or not an MJ 12 committee had ever been formed. The response came back negative. However, Good commented that AFOSI is an agency whose work involves counterintelligence and deception, and carries a longtime involvement in the UFO agenda. Moore would later claim that Colonel Barry Hennessey of AFOSI directed the entire New Mexico disinformation scheme at the Pentagon. It seems the Roswell story has changed at every turn, depending on whose voice is speaking.

And, it changed again when more documents surfaced on March 14, 1994, delivered to long-time UFOlogist Dan Berliner. Like Shandera's account, Berliner said he received two undeveloped rolls of film in the mail from an anonymous source. Inside, he found photos of copied pages from a "Top Secret/MAJIC/Eyes Only" special operations manual labeled "SOM 1 01." The records detailed how military crews should recover crashed saucers and their extraterrestrial crews,

*The B-2 Spirit Stealth Bomber, some claim, is the product of reverse-engineering*

"SOME TESTIMONIES INDICATE THAT ONE OF THE ALIEN CREW SURVIVED AND IS NOW A RESIDENT OF 'HANGAR 18' AT WRIGHT-PATTERSON. APPARENTLY, THIS ALIEN IS ALIVE AND TREATED AS AN HONORED GUEST AT THE BASE, ACTING AS A LIAISON BETWEEN THE GOVERNMENT AND THE EXTRATERRESTRIAL COMMUNITY."

and instructed all remains to be shipped to "Area 51." Area 51 is a remote tract of land in southern Nevada at the edge of Groom Lake. It contains an airfield whose primary purpose is believed to be the operation and analysis of enemy aircraft and weapons systems. It is also thought to promote secret development and testing of new military aircraft.

Several witness accounts testify that debris from Roswell was indeed shipped to Area 51. Conspiracy theorists claim that the weightless material first discovered by Major Marcel is reportedly being used for the purpose of reverse engineering. By studying the alien technology, they say, American scientists and engineers have achieved technological advances far earlier than expected. They point to the construction of aircraft such as the stealth bomber as an example. In his controversial

book *The Day After Roswell*, Colonel Philip J. Corso (U.S. Army, retired) maintains that he distributed artifacts recovered at Roswell to select government contractors. Corso's credentials cannot be overlooked. He served on Eisenhower's security council, and then on the Army Research and Development Department's Foreign Technology Desk at the Pentagon.

Other witnesses claim that between three and five bodies were found at the Roswell crash. They have been described as small, hairless beings with large heads and round, oddly spaced eyes. The Eisenhower memo mentions the human-like bodies, but states that all four were declared dead. In their book *UFO Crash at Roswell*, Don Schmidt and Kevin Randle include an interview with General Arthur Exon who says that the corpses were transferred to Wright-Patterson Air Force Base in Dayton, Ohio. Some testimonies indicate that one of the alien crew survived and is now a resident of "Hangar 18" at Wright-Patterson. Apparently, this alien is alive and treated as an honored guest at the base, acting as a liaison between the government and the extraterrestrial community.

Meanwhile, the government claims that the "alien bodies" were actually test dummies, roughly the size of humans, used in the experiment. The weather balloon was apparently a top-secret intelligence-gathering device that required an initial cover-up for the purpose of National Security. So where does the truth lie? In 1997, a CNN/Time poll was taken to commemorate the 10th anniversary of the Roswell event. It indicated that 80 percent of the American public believes that the government is withholding information about the UFO mystery. Perhaps, in due time, more documents will surface that will lead us closer to the answer. 

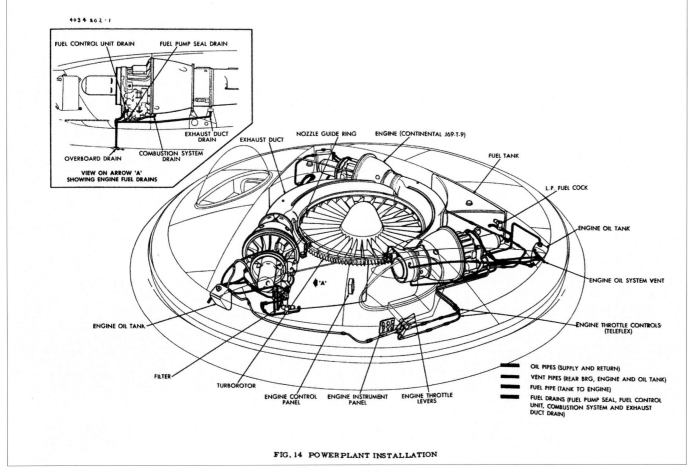

FIG. 14 POWERPLANT INSTALLATION

*The Avrocar was an actual "flying saucer" aircraft developed as part of a secret U.S. military project in 1958-1959*

CHAPTER 10:

# THE BILDERBERG GROUP

A GROUP FORMED OF INDUSTRIALISTS, BANKERS, MEDIA KINGPINS AND POLITICIANS. THE VENUE, ATTENDEES AND DISCUSSIONS ARE KEPT SECRET, FUELLING THEORIES OF A "SHADOW GOVERNMENT."

To what extent do private groups control the levers of global power? The mysterious Bilderberg Group, for one, gives rise to this question. It has become a target of increasing public scrutiny.

This most powerful group of businessmen and world leaders first met in 1954 at The Bilderberg Hotel in the Dutch town of Oosterbeck. It was a meeting held in secret, reserved for the invitation-only guest list. They gathered to discuss the political climate in a post-World War II environment. For the next 53 years, the highly selective group has continued to meet and has been accused of fixing the world's fate behind closed doors. It has grown into an annual event attended by the power-elite of the world's leading industrialists, bankers, politicians, and media moguls. However, the venues, attendees, and subjects discussed are not disclosed to the public. It is proof, say the conspiracy theorists, that there indeed exists a shadowy global government pulling the strings.

*Boating in Leiden, Holland*

" THE COMMITTEE HAS DISPLAYED A REMARKABLE ABILITY FOR IDENTIFYING NEW TALENT. IT IS SAID THAT BILL CLINTON ATTENDED IN 1991, WHILE STILL GOVERNOR OF ARKANSAS, AND TONY BLAIR SHOWED UP TWO YEARS LATER, WELL IN ADVANCE OF BECOMING BRITAIN'S PRIME MINISTER."

Each year the Bilderberg "steering committee" compiles a guest list of approximately 100 names, extending invitations only to residents of North America and Europe. While the list has never been publicly released, the roster of names is routinely published by an anonymous source. Regular participants have reportedly included luminaries such as Henry Kissinger and former UK Chancellor of the Exchequer Kenneth Clarke. Furthermore, the committee has displayed a remarkable ability for identifying new talent. It is said that Bill Clinton attended in 1991, while still governor of Arkansas, and Tony Blair showed up two years later, well in advance of becoming

Britain's Prime Minister. Close observers of the group say other past attendees have included Presidents and Vice Presidents of the United States, Directors of the CIA and the FBI, General Secretaries of NATO, American Senators and members of Congress, European Prime Ministers, as well as Presidents of the International Monetary Fund, The World Bank and Federal Reserve. Reports also list Chairmen of the 100 most powerful corporations in the world, representing DaimlerChrysler, Coca Cola, British Petroleum, Chase Manhattan Bank, American Express, Goldman Sachs, and Microsoft.

While The Bilderberg Group avoids the stereotypical traits of secret societies, such as secret rites and rituals, it certainly ranks high on mystique. It is widely reported that top editors and CEOs of the leading newspapers in the world participate, and yet nothing is ever printed in the media. Not a single word has ever been breathed about what has been discussed at these meetings. When the Davos World Economic Forum and G8 meetings are getting front-page coverage, it is no surprise then that suspicions are growing about what the Bilderbergers are really up to.

It is the secrecy that many argue is antithetical to the democratic ideals of public debate. "Any modern democratic system protects the right to privacy," says Daniel Estulin, author of The True History of Club Bilderberg, "but doesn't the public have a right to know what their political leaders are talking about when they meet the wealthiest business leaders of their respective countries?" If the Bilderbergers are functioning for the good of society, Estulin underlines, then why is their society so secret?

Etienne Davignon, the group's current Chairman, prefers to use the term "private" to describe the network, as opposed to "secret."

*Co-founder Prince Bernhard of The Netherlands*

Bill Clinton is said to have attended the 1991 Bildeburg meeting while still Governor of Arkansas

"BILDEBERG SUPPORTERS BELIEVE ITS PRIVATE NETWORKS ARE CRUCIAL TO THE SUCCESS OF MODERN DEMOCRACY."

The NATO flag

"THE ORIGINAL INTENTION OF THE BILDERBERG GROUP, IN FACT, WAS TO PROMOTE COMMUNICATION AND UNDERSTANDING BETWEEN WESTERN EUROPE AND NORTH AMERICA THROUGH INFORMAL MEETINGS."

A corporate director and former European Commissioner, Davignon explains that discretion is necessary to allow members to speak freely "off the record" in order to avoid using the language of a press release. He scoffs at the allegations that Bilderberg is a global conspiracy secretly ruling the world. "It is unavoidable, and it doesn't matter," he said in a rare 2005 interview with the BBC. "There will always be people who believe in conspiracies but things happen in a much more incoherent fashion." The goal, as he describes it, is to create an environment where persons of influence can share ideas in a way that allows the debate to be completely open. Some supporters believe such private networks are crucial to the success of modern democracy. "There needs to be places where these people can think about the main challenges ahead, coordinate where policies should be going, and find out where there could be a consensus," says Professor Kees van der Piil of Sussex University in Britain.

The original intention of the Bilderberg Group, in fact, was to promote communication and understanding between Western Europe and North America through informal meetings. It was founded by Joseph Retinger, who persuaded Prince Bernhard of The Netherlands to host a secret conference for representatives of NATO countries. A Polish émigré and political advisor, Retinger had been instrumental in launching the Council of Europe in 1949, and believed in creating forums where long-term concerns would not be upstaged by short-term

agendas between governments. Attendees at the first conference included the director of the CIA, representatives from the Rockefeller family, and U.S. General Walter Bedell Smith. It was so successful that Retinger was appointed the group's first permanent secretary, and Prince Bernhard took on the role of Chairman until 1976, when he resigned due to his involvement with the Lockheed scandal. It was revealed that Prince Bernhard had accepted a US $1.1 million bribe from the U.S. aircraft manufacturer to influence the Dutch government's purchase of its fighter jet. There was no conference that year—the only exception to date.

The 2007 Bilderberg meeting reportedly took place in Istanbul, Turkey at the Ritz Carlton. The "official" guest list has since been leaked, naming Richard Haas (President, Council of Foreign Relations), Paul Wolfowitz (former President of the World Bank) and Bernard Koucher (France's newly appointed Minister of Foreign Affairs). As usual, the media was present in full force, including representatives from *The International Herald Tribune*, *The Economist* and *The Washington Post*, each one putting down his pen and notepad for the occasion. The question is: what was discussed? Many speculate the key topics included the Iraq War and the world's energy crisis. Others presume attendees were more interested in the propagation of their own interests at the expense of global concerns. Regardless, those on the outside will remain outsiders, and will never know.

The Bilderberg Group was created in 1954 as a forum for representatives from NATO countries

*Leiden, Holland, the site of the Bilderberg headquarters*

# "PROTESTERS ACCUSE THE BILDERBERG GROUP OF BEING A SUPRA-GOVERNMENTAL ORGANIZATION"

Istanbul, Turkey was the reported location of the 2007 Bilderberg conference

More and more, protesters are demanding to be let in. They are accusing the Bilderberg Group of being a supra-governmental organization, manipulating currencies and monetary rates, and deciding which countries will wage war on others. Some suspect that the Bilderbergers also have their hands deep in the election process. These objectors, however, offer no definitive proof to support their claims. At the same time, as Estulin argues, "what guarantees do citizens have that the Bilderberg Club isn't a center for influence trafficking and lobbying if they aren't allowed to know what their representatives talk about at the Club's secret gatherings?"

While the charges may seem far-fetched, little information is available about the Bilderberg Group that would alleviate concerns. The organization operates out of a small office in Leiden, Holland, which is managed by a single person using one telephone line. If you make a telephone inquiry, you are likely to get an electronic voice asking you to leave a message. If you do a search on the Internet, you will find no website. C. Gordon Tether, a journalist for the *Financial Times*, may have put it best. On May 6, 1975, he wrote: "If the Bilderberg Group is not a conspiracy of some sort, it is conducted in such a way as to give a remarkably good imitation of one."

# CHAPTER 11:

# PRIORY OF SION

EITHER A SOCIETY FOUNDED TO PRESERVE

THE BLOODLINE OF JESUS CHRIST

—OR A 20TH-CENTURY HOAX BASED

ON A SERIES OF FORGERIES.

Jesus on the cross

Suppose that Jesus Christ had never been crucified. What if, instead, he and Mary Magdalene had escaped together to France? Suppose that they then bore a child, whose existence and offspring have since been hidden from the world.

It is hard to imagine such a scenario, which would overturn the entire foundation of Christianity. And yet, a lengthy list of Christ's descendants can indeed be found in "secret files" housed at the Bibliothèque Nationale in Paris, citing such prominent figures as Leonardo da Vinci, Victor Hugo and Isaac Newton. Allegedly, the Priory of Sion is the secret society founded to protect and preserve this bloodline. While some say it has existed since the Crusades, others claim it is a bona fide 20th century hoax. Where does the truth lie?

To uncover the mystery behind this secret order, you must first travel to a small, remote village in the foothills of the French Pyrénées called Rennes le Château. There, the story begins with François Bérenger Saunière, a parish priest considered controversial for his rants against the French Republic. In 1885, he received a penal displacement to this township of not more than 200 inhabitants. Saunière set about renovating his church, Sainte Marie Madeleine, in the company of his housekeeper Marie Denarnaud. Over the next ten years, he also built the Tower of Magdala in honor of Mary Magdalene as well as a mansion for himself and Marie called Villa Bethania. It is estimated that Saunière spent 200,000 francs for these construction projects, the equivalent of US $1.25 million. People began to question where Saunière had acquired his financing. Rumors started to spread that he had found a medieval treasure buried beneath the church.

The gossip eventually reached the local Catholic bishop, who investigated the matter.

A stained-glass window depicting Jesus on the cross

*Statue of Blanche de Castille*

He concluded that Saunière had in fact made his money from "trafficking the Masses," a common transgression among 19th and 20th century priests. At the time, custom dictated that priests received a fixed stipend for each Mass. However, some priests exploited their position by taking on additional services, thereby accumulating great financial rewards. This scheme created competition among priests that was condemned by the Church. The Bishop quickly determined that Saunière was compensated for many more Masses than he could feasibly have officiated, and promptly defrocked him in 1909.

Before his death in 1917, Saunière had transferred Villa Bethania to Marie, by then assumed to be his lover. In the early 1950s,

the hearsay about a buried treasured resurfaced when she was looking to sell the property. Noel Corbu bought it and converted the house into a hotel called "Hôtel de la Tour." Corbu used the press to promote the legend, thereby attracting a sizable clientele. He spun tales that Saunière had found the treasure of Blanche de Castille, the wife of King Louis VIII. His business boomed. People arrived in droves, with axes and spades in hand, looking to test their luck.

Pierre Plantard caught wind of this fascinating tale. An admirer of Adolf Hitler, this Parisian native had been the leader of minor occult groups, aiming to purify France from Jewish and Masonic influences. His organization "Alpha Galates" published *Circuit*, a magazine that carried stories about

*Rennes-le-Château*

*Bibliothèque Nationale de Paris*

Saunière and his mysterious findings. After exchanging letters with Corbu, Plantard took the story of Rennes le Château to new heights. He announced that Saunière had not only unearthed valuable antiquities, but also the body of Jesus Christ. According to Plantard, Jesus did not die on the cross, as Christianity would have you believe. Instead, he married Mary Magdalene and moved to France. The divine couple had children now traceable through the Merovingian family line, the first non-Roman rulers of Gaul. Their descendants then went underground, preserved by a secret organization called The Priory of Sion. This Order was dedicated to restoring the Merovingian dynasty to the throne of France. Plantard went on to suggest that he was not only the current Grand Master of the Priory, but also the last descendant of the Merovingians.

Plantard manufactured evidence to support his story. In 1956, he registered "The Priory of Sion" as an association in the French town of Annemasse. He claimed it was an offshoot of the "Order of Sion," a monastic order founded during the Crusades. Modern historians remain highly skeptical on this point. The medieval order carries no link to Rennes le Château or the Merovingian dynasty. Then, in the 1960s, Plantard began writing a manuscript that included medieval parchments, forged by Philippe de Chérisy, to make a case for the Priory's authenticity. Plantard would later claim that Saunière discovered the documents while renovating his church. Together, these two men fabricated a legend of monstrous proportions. Plantard eventually enlisted the help of author Gérard de Sède to write a book based on his manuscript. In 1967, *L'Or de Renne* (The Gold of Rennes) became a popular title in France. Many readers took the story seriously, assuming that the phony documents were in fact centuries old.

Then, in 1975, Plantard and de Chérisy deposited a series of forged documents at the Bibliothèque Nationale (National Library) de Paris, the so-called *"Dossiers Secrets d'Henri Lobineau."* A British researcher by the name of Henry Lincoln came across the "evidence," which included genealogical tables linking Jesus Christ to the Merovingians and Plantard. Lincoln subsequently persuaded the BBC to produce a documentary about the mysteries of Rennes le Château. He continued to expand on the conspiracy theories by writing his own

books. Lincoln then joined forces with co-authors Michael Baigent and Richard Leigh to produce the landmark novel *Holy Blood, Holy Grail*. The book drew on Plantard's source documents, which the book portrayed as fact. The tall tale spun an endless yarn that stimulated great public response.

Eventually, it was revealed that the "secret files" were forgeries. Plantard's criminal record was also exposed, having been previously convicted of fraud and embezzlement. In 1989, Plantard attempted to salvage his reputation by

Leonardo da Vinci, alleged to be the Priory of Sion's 12th Grand Master

"PIERRE PLANTARD CAUGHT WIND OF THIS FASCINATING TALE. AN ADMIRER OF ADOLF HITLER, THIS PARISIAN NATIVE HAD BEEN THE LEADER OF MINOR OCCULT GROUPS, AIMING TO PURIFY FRANCE FROM JEWISH AND MASONIC INFLUENCES. PLANTARD TOOK THE STORY OF RENNES LE CHÂTEAU TO NEW HEIGHTS."

*Pierre Plantard registered the Priory of Sion in 1956, thereby fabricating what is now considered to be a notorious hoax*

declaring that the Priory of Sion had in fact been founded in 1681 at Rennes le Château. He wanted to disassociate himself from the discredited version, and in turn, produced a second list of Grand Masters. Plantard would then only dig his hole deeper. In 1993, he claimed that Roger Patrice Pelat had once been a Grand Master of the Priory of Sion. Pelat had died in 1989 during an investigation for insider trading, and had also been a friend of the then-French President François Mitterrand. When Plantard made his announcement, Pelat's name was associated with a current investigation involving French Prime Minister Pierre Bérégovoy.

Plantard's interference with the law led the French authorities to search his home. They discovered a bunch of harmless documents, among which Plantard proclaimed himself the true King of France. Under oath, Plantard admitted that he had fabricated everything. He was ordered to cease all activities and lived in obscurity until his death in 2000.

Today, modern scholars refer to the Priory of Sion as a notorious hoax. French authors have detailed their conclusions, reporting evidence that more sensational writers have conveniently ignored. The evidence includes correspondence between Plantard, de Chérisy and de Sède detailing the strategy behind their conspiracy. Dating from the 1960s, these 100-plus letters are now in the hands of French researcher Jean-Luc Chaumeil, who has written numerous books and articles exposing Plantard and his secret order.

More recently, Dan Brown's bestseller *The Da Vinci Code* and its movie adaptation have spurred renewed interest in the Priory of Sion. The novel begins with the murder of the Priory's Grand Master, curiously named "Saunière." According to the premise, the Holy Grail is not a physical chalice, but a woman, namely Mary Magdalene, who carried the bloodline of Christ. The Priory of Sion reportedly hid the Grail relics in a secret crypt, the discovery of which would shake the very foundation of Christianity. Brown himself perpetuates the underlying myth saying that, "the secret behind *The Da Vinci Code* was too well documented and significant for me to dismiss."

Perhaps the one thing more powerful than a secret society is our desire to believe in one. "Even if there is no treasure of any kind whatsoever to be found there," says Jean-Luc Chaumeil about Rennes le Château, "each human being can still undertake a personal quest there, a recharging of their batteries, as it were."

*The "Apprentice Pillar" at Rosslyn Chapel*

# FURTHER INFORMATION

## BOOKS:

- *Above Top Secret*, by Timothy Good
- *A History of Secret Societies*, by Arkon Daraul
- *American Freemasons*, by Mark Tabbert
- *America's Secret Establishment: An Introduction to the Order of Skull & Bones*, by Anthony Sutton
- *Case MJ-12: The True Story Behind the Government's UFO Conspiracies*, by Kevin Randle
- *Conspiracies and Secret Societies*, by Brad & Sherry Steiger
- *The Day After Roswell*, by Philip J. Corso
- *History of the Order of Assassins*, by Enno Franzius
- *The Klan*, by Patsy Sims
- *The Klan Unmasked*, by Stetson Kennedy
- *Ku Klux Klan: America's First Terrorists*, by Patrick O'Donnell & David Jacobs
- *The Knights Templar: The Essential History*, by Stephen Howarth
- *The Origins of Freemasonry: Facts and Fictions*, by Margaret C. Jacob

- *The Real Roswell Crashed Saucer Cover-up*, by Philip Klass
- *The Rosicrucians: The History, Rituals and Mythology of an Esoteric Order*, by Christopher McIntosh
- *Secrets of the Tombs: Skull and Bones, the Ivy League, and the Hidden Paths of Power*, by Alexandra Robbins
- *Secret Societies: Inside the World's Most Notorious Organizations*, by John Lawrence Reynolds
- *Secret Societies of All Ages and Countries*, by Charles William Heckethorn
- *The True History of Club Bilderberg*, by Daniel Estulin
- *UFO Crash at Roswell*, by Kevin Randle and Don Schmidtt
- *Who Rules America?* by G. William Dumhoff

## FILMS:

- *Blood in the Face*, documentary by James Ridgeway
- *World History of Organized Crime*, documentary produced by The History Channel
- *Mafia: The History of the Mob in America*, documentary produced by A&E

## WEB SITES:

The Ancient Mystical Order Rosae Crucis
**http://www.amorc.org/**

Committee for Skeptical Inquiry
**http://www.csicop.org/**

Grand Lodge of Freemasons in Massachusetts
**http://www.massfreemasonry.org/**

Prince Hall Grand Lodge
**http://www.princehall.org/**

The United Grand Lodge of England
**http://www.grandlodge-england.org/**

# INDEX

ITEMS WITH THEIR OWN CHAPTER ARE SHOWN IN BOLD